Access to History

General Editor: Keith Randel.

July
1999

Britain and the European Powers

1865-1914

Access to History

General Editor: Keith Randell

Britain and the European Powers 1865-1914

Robert Pearce

Hodder & Stoughton

A MEMBER OF THE HODDER HEADLINE GROUP

Some other titles in the series:

The Habsburg Empire Nicholas Pelling	ISBN 0 340 59377 6
The British Empire 1815-1914 Frank McDonough	ISBN 0 340 59376 8
The Concert of Europe: International Relations 1814-70 John Lowe	ISBN 0 340 53496 6
Rivalry and Accord: International Relations 1870-1914 John Lowe	ISBN 0 340 51806 5
France: The Third Republic 1870-1914 Keith Randell	ISBN 0 340 55569 6
Reaction and Revolutions: Russia 1881-1924 Michael Lynch	ISBN 0 340 53336 6
From Bismarck to Hitler: Germany 1890-1933 Geoff Layton	ISBN 0 340 59488 8

British Library Cataloguing in Publication Data

A catalogue for this title is available from the British Library

ISBN 0-340-64327-7

First published 1996

Impression number	10	9	8	7	6	5	4	3	2	1
Year	1999		1998		1997		1996			

Copyright © 1996 Robert Pearce

Typeset by Sempringham publishing services, Bedford
Printed in Great Britain for Hodder & Stoughton Educational,
a division of Hodder Headline Plc, 338 Euston Road, London NW1 3BH
by Redwood Books, Trowbridge, Wiltshire

Contents

CHAPTER 1 Introduction: Britain and the European Powers   1
  1 Britain around 1865   1
  2 The Eastern Question and the Crimean War   3
  3 Conditions after 1865   6
  4 Foreign Policy after 1865: an Overview   8
  Study Guides   12

CHAPTER 2 Disraeli and Foreign Policy, 1865-80   14
  1 Foreign Policy from 1865-74   14
  2 The Impact of Disraeli   16
  3 Disraeli and the Eastern Question, 1875-6   17
  4 The 'Bulgarian Horrors'   19
  5 The Russo-Turkish War   22
  6 The Congress of Berlin   27
  7 Imperial Troubles   32
  8 Conclusion   34
  Study Guides   37

CHAPTER 3 The Foreign Policy of Gladstone, 1880-94   42
  1 The 1880 General Election   42
  2 The Impact of Gladstone: Change and Continuity   43
  3 Turkey   46
  4 Afghanistan   47
  5 South Africa   48
  6 Egypt   52
  7 Imperial Expansion   59
  8 Foreign Policy in 1886 and 1892-4   60
  9 Conclusion   60
  Study Guides   66

CHAPTER 4 'Splendid Isolation' and its Demise, 1885-1907   70
  1 Lord Salisbury and Foreign Policy   70
  2 Salisbury's Foreign Policies, 1885-92   72
  3 Salisbury's Policies, 1895-1902   76
  4 The Diplomatic 'Revolution' of 1902-7   82
  Study Guides   90

CHAPTER 5 Britain and the Origins of the First World War   93
  1 The Climate of Opinion   93
  2 Anglo-German Antagonism   97
  3 British Foreign Policy, 1912-14   106
  4 The Outbreak of War   108
  5 Conclusion   113
  Study Guides   116

CHAPTER 6 Conclusion   121
        1   Change and Continuity in British Foreign Policy   121
        2   Serving the National Interest?   126

        Chronological Table   129

        Further Reading   132

        Index   134

Preface

To the general reader

Although the *Access to History* series has been designed with the needs of students studying the subject at higher examination levels very much in mind, it also has a great deal to offer the general reader. The main body of the text (i.e. ignoring the Study Guides at the ends of chapters) forms a readable and yet stimulating survey of a coherent topic as studied by historians. However, each author's aim has not merely been to provide a clear explanation of what happened in the past (to interest and inform): it has also been assumed that most readers wish to be stimulated into thinking further about the topic and to form opinions of their own about the significance of the events that are described and discussed (to be challenged). Thus, although no prior knowledge of the topic is expected on the reader's part, she or he is treated as an intelligent and thinking person throughout. The author tends to share ideas and possibilities with the reader, rather than passing on numbers of so-called 'historical truths'.

To the student reader

There are many ways in which the series can be used by students studying History at a higher level. It will, therefore, be worthwhile thinking about your own study strategy before you start your work on this book. Obviously, your strategy will vary depending on the aim you have in mind, and the time for study that is available to you.

If, for example, you want to acquire a general overview of the topic in the shortest possible time, the following approach will probably be the most effective:

1 Read Chapter 1 and think about its contents.
2 Read the 'Making notes' section at the end of Chapter 2 and decide whether it is necessary for you to read this chapter.
3 If it is, read the chapter, stopping at each heading to note down the main points that have been made.
4 Repeat stage 2 (and stage 3 where appropriate) for all the other chapters.

If, however, your aim is to gain a thorough grasp of the topic, taking however much time is necessary to do so, you may benefit from carrying out the same procedure with each chapter, as follows:

1 Read the chapter as fast as you can, and preferably at one sitting.
2 Study the flow diagram at the end of the chapter, ensuring that you understand the general 'shape' of what you have just read.

Preface

3 Read the 'Making notes' section (and the 'Answering essay questions' section, if there is one) and decide what further work you need to do on the chapter. In particularly important sections of the book, this will involve reading the chapter a second time and stopping at each heading to think about (and to write a summary of) what you have just read.
4 Attempt the 'Source-based questions' section. It will sometimes be sufficient to think through your answers, but additional understanding will often be gained by forcing yourself to write them down.

When you have finished the main chapters of the book, study the 'Further Reading' section and decide what additional reading (if any) you will do on the topic.

This book has been designed to help make your studies both enjoyable and successful. If you can think of ways in which this could have been done more effectively, please write to tell me. In the meantime, I hope that you will gain greatly from your study of History.

Keith Randell

Acknowledgements

The Publishers would like to thank the following for permission to reproduce illustrations in this volume:

Cover - Robert Gascoyne-Cecil, 3rd Marquess of Salisbury, by Sir John Everett Millais. Reproduced by courtesy of the National Portrait Gallery, London. Punch Publications pp. 21, 29, 51, 99, 100 and 112; The Gladstone ABC p. 54.

The Publishers would also like to thank the following for permission to reproduce copyright material:

Oxford University Press for extracts from *The Foreign Policy of Victorian England*, by Kenneth Bourne, (1970); Macmillan Publishers Ltd. for an extract from *Africa and the Victorians*, by J.C. Gallagher, (1965); Athlone Press for an extract from *Lord Salisbury and Foreign Policy*, by J.A.S. Grenville, (1964).

Every effort has been made to trace and acknowledge ownership of copyright. The Publishers will be glad to make suitable arrangements with any copyright holders whom it has not been possible to contact.

CHAPTER 1

Introduction: Britain and the European Powers

1 Britain around 1865

In 1865 Lord Palmerston died. He was mourned as one of the outstanding foreign secretaries of the nineteenth century, a symbol of Britain's greatness in the world. As *The Times* obituary put it, he had been 'the terror of the Continent'. Prophets of doom were convinced that, without him, things would never be the same again; but most politically conscious Victorians believed that their country's greatness rested on secure foundations. Was not Britain's economy the strongest in the world and its empire the largest?

The first country to undergo substantial industrial growth, Britain had the most advanced industrial economy in the world around 1865 and was also the most urbanised nation on earth. So far was Britain ahead of her rivals that she enjoyed unchallenged supremacy in world manufacturing output.

Economic Output of the Great Powers, 1870 (millions of tons)

	Coal	Iron	Percent of World Manufacturing Output
Britain	112.0	6.0	22
France	23.0	1.2	8
Germany	34.0	1.3	5
Russia	0.7	0.4	7
U.S.A.	10.0	1.7	8

Even these figures do not tell the whole story, for British shipping dominated world commerce, while the City of London was banker and moneylender to the rest of the world.

In consequence, some were complacent, even smug, about the superiority of all things British. To them, there seemed something slightly ridiculous about foreigners - they were, in the words of a Dickens character, quite simply a 'mistake'. Queen Victoria believed that the British were 'the only honest people, and therefore our task in dealing with others who are not so is dreadful'. It was almost distasteful to the Victorians to have a foreign policy at all. But someone had to keep troublesome foreigners in order, and who better than the British?

a) A Satisfied Power

It might be imagined that such economic and financial dominance would be translated into an aggressive external policy. After all, as A.J.P. Taylor once commented, 'Powers will be Powers'! Certainly Britain had the largest empire the world had ever seen. Its total population, excluding the United Kingdom's, was 235 million, covering almost eight million square miles in five continents. It was the empire 'upon which the sun never sets'. In addition, Palmerston as Foreign Secretary had been renowned for his 'gunboat diplomacy'. This was a man who would stand no nonsense in asserting British rights wherever they were challenged in the world. Yet several commentators noted that the targets of his wrath were carefully chosen opponents, usually much weaker. He stood off from greater challenges, knowing full well that although Britain's navy was the strongest in the world, and had been since the defeat of Napoleon in 1815, its army was relatively weak. Why were the Victorians not more aggressive in their foreign policy?

There are several answers to this question:

i) Britain was a wealthy and powerful country with a large empire. It had already been aggressive: now there was a perceived need for consolidation. What need was there for extra territory? Already economic influence, verging on dominance, was spreading without the necessity for 'formal empire' (with administrative costs and the troublesome need to station troops to keep the native inhabitants in order). In short, Britain was a satisfied Power. Many Britons, indeed, believed that the only proper aims of foreign policy were the promotion of peace. War might be necessary to protect the British Isles and the Empire, but it was not to be entered into lightly.

ii) Undue aggression might lead to the formation of a combination of Powers against Britain. This had happened in the past to Spain and France, and it could happen again.

iii) War was economically harmful. It would disrupt world trade, from which Britain benefited so much, and would therefore be bad for business. Furthermore, war would play havoc with the financial and economic policies which, it was widely believed, had helped to produce wealth in the first place. Britain's spectacular success was thought to have arisen from the free play of economic forces: governments stood aside and allowed entrepreneurs to use their talent, inventiveness and hard work to produce the goods which the world wanted to buy. Official policy was therefore *laissez-faire:* the less government, the better. Yet war, being so costly, would entail high rates of taxation and so might well lead to severe economic problems.

b) Foreign Policy Options

British foreign policy and defence, therefore, had to be relatively cheap, and between 1815 and 1865 defence expenditure averaged only two or three per cent of gross national product. Palmerston knew that the Royal Navy was supreme at sea and that it could bombard ports, but what of fighting on land? He always insisted that, in the last analysis, Britain's strength lay not in her existing fighting forces but in her potential for raising massive forces in an emergency. Hence there was always an element of uncertainty - perhaps of bluff - attaching to Britain's real power in foreign policy terms. Since major wars were shunned, no one could be quite sure of her strength. Was Britannia really arrayed in a fine new suit of clothes or was she naked?

As a result of these factors, there were those in Britain who favoured outright isolation. This view was put forward most eloquently by the radicals Richard Cobden and John Bright. They believed that Britain should set an example of tolerance and peace. 'Free trade' was their policy and their maxim. They believed that countries which traded together, without any restrictions or barriers, would get on well together. Under free trade a world community would be created: nations would specialise in what they did best, and therefore they would be dependent upon each other for the many goods which they did not themselves produce. Hence it would be economic madness for countries to go to war with trading partners, on whom they relied for their economic well-being. Similarly, there would be no need for colonies, for every nation would have access to raw materials at the market price, and so imperialism, another cause of international friction, would be rendered obsolete. In fact, in their view, free trade would render a foreign policy virtually unnecessary. Admittedly wars had sometimes resulted from the search for prestige in the past, but this aristocratic quest was altogether too childish for the second half of the nineteenth century. At least this is what the idealists hoped.

Most people did not go this far, and indeed some wanted to achieve spectacular foreign policy successes. But many - and perhaps most - Victorians thought that Britain should pursue a peaceful course in international affairs, focusing first on the defence of Britain and its Empire and intervening in European affairs only reluctantly to ensure that problems were solved in a quick and business-like manner. The two main methods of settling Europe's problems were (i) by agreement among the Great Powers, using the so-called 'Concert of Europe', and (ii) by throwing Britain's weight into a coalition against a potential aggressor, thus ensuring the 'balance of power'. Most Britons were prepared to use either of these methods, when it was necessary to intervene at all.

2 The Eastern Question and the Crimean War

To desire peace and the maintenance of the *status quo* was easy, but to avoid war was often very difficult, given that Europe was in a state of flux. In 1854 Britain, together with France, joined the Crimean War against Russia. The precise details of the conflict fall outside the scope of this book (see *Britain and the European Powers, 1815-65* in this series);

but the fundamental issues at stake, and the peace settlement, were vital for foreign policy after 1865.

The main problem was the Eastern Question, i.e. what to do about the declining Ottoman (Turkish) Empire. Founded in earlier centuries, when Turkey had been much stronger, the Empire covered a vast area, including present-day Turkey, much of North Africa and the Balkans, and contained an explosive mixture of races and religions. By the middle of the nineteenth century the grip of the Turkish overlords was extremely weak. Already Greece had broken away, and Serbia and Montenegro had become autonomous (see the map on page 5). Indeed it was the Balkan region which saw most instability around this time. Ottoman rule here had, for a long time, served several useful purposes. To the British, it acted as a useful buffer to Russian expansion, while to the Russians it checked the growth of British imperial influence. For Austria (a multi-racial empire), it prevented the menacing emergence of independent states composed of the same racial groups (known, broadly, as Slavs) as its own subject peoples. The disintegration of the Ottoman empire would therefore be very dangerous indeed to Austria: it might produce not only new Balkan states but, eventually, the break-up of the Austrian empire, if independent Slav states proved attractive enough to its subject races. If the Ottoman Empire did not exist, it was said, it would be necessary to invent it, so many useful purposes did it serve. But could it survive much longer? It was in this period that many people were urging that the old dynastic empires (based, theoretically, upon the notion that God had parcelled out the earth to his representatives, and thus upon the 'divine right of kings') lacked legitimacy: nationalists were insisting, instead, that states should be based on a sense of common identity and that, in consequence, the old empires of Europe should be broken up into smaller nation states. Nationalism was a growing force after 1850, and it was threatening the overthrow of the old dynastic empires. Turkish rule, it seemed, might be the first to be replaced, followed by Austrian.

Most European states disliked Turkish rule in the Balkans: it meant Muslim rule over Christians, and furthermore it was generally inefficient and cruel administration. Yet the European Powers feared the upheaval that was likely to accompany its disintegration, and Britain, Austria and Russia had for some time endorsed Turkish rule. However, Russia was ambivalent: the dominant people in Russia were Slavs, who had much in common with the Balkan races, leading to the growth of 'Panslavism', a movement for the political union, or at least mutual support, of all Slavs (despite the fact that they had religious and language differences). The Tsar also felt it necessary, as head of the Orthodox Church, to champion his co-religionists under Muslim rule. In addition, the Russians considered the Balkans a vital area strategically. Access to the Mediterranean Sea via the Straits (the Bosphorus and the Dardanelles) was vital to the Russian economy, since none of their northern ports could be kept free of ice, and open to traffic, for the whole year. A cardinal principle of Russian policy, therefore, was that Constantinople and the Straits had to be either in weak Turkish hands or placed under direct Russian control: if any other Power controlled them, Russia might suffer 'economic strangulation'.

In 1853 religious quarrels led the Tsar to demand recognition as protector of Turkey's Christian subjects, arousing opposition from Britain and France, who objected to increased Russian influence in the Near East. Diplomatic blunders saw the escalation of the crisis to produce the Crimean War in 1854. Britain and France emerged victorious in 1856, when a threat of war from Austria (formerly Russia's trusted ally) induced the Russians to call for peace. But neither side had performed well militarily, both exhibiting administrative chaos on a

The Balkans, circa 1865

grand scale.

Luckily for Britain, this test of its Great Power status did not continue for longer. The war was ended in 1856 by the Congress of Paris, whose terms set the contours of British policy for the next two decades. Russia, as the defeated party, lost small amounts of territory and renounced claims for a religious protectorate over Turkish Christians. Most important of all, the Black Sea was neutralised (and was henceforth open to all merchant ships but no warships) and the independence of the Turkish Empire was guaranteed by the Great Powers, including Britain.

Britain had saddled itself with a severe problem by this action. She had guaranteed an empire (popularly known as the 'Sick Man of Europe') which was patently decaying. Nor did the Ottoman Sultan - an enormous glutton and the keeper of a harem with hundreds of concubines - attempt to reform his lands. Why should he, now that he was assured of Great Power support?

3 Conditions after 1865

After the Crimean War a reaction set in. The unpleasant taste of war reinforced the traditional British preference for peace, and there was now an inclination to avoid foreign entanglements. Yet this was not so easy. Not only had Britain guaranteed the independence of Turkey, but her worldwide interests created plenty of opportunities for problems with other Powers. There were many sources of friction after 1865.

British foreign policy was now conditioned by several patent weaknesses. Britain had interests all over the world, not only because of the scattered nature of her large empire but because she had foreign investments virtually everywhere. Thus she was hampered in relations with European Powers by being more committed than they, and perhaps indeed over-stretched. And despite being economically more powerful than any other state, it was soon apparent that the 1860s saw the summit of this dominance. A Power at the zenith can only decline.

a) Relative Economic Decline

It soon became apparent that economic rivals were catching up with Great Britain. In 1865 civil war ended in the United States of America, boosting that country's production; and in 1871 the states of 'Germany' (until then little more than a geographical expression) became unified into a single state, also enhancing economic growth. Britain's economy still continued to expand, but now these naturally wealthier countries (with larger populations and richer natural resources) began to grow more quickly. It was relatively simple for other states to copy the industrial processes first begun in Britain, especially since British investments abroad served to speed up this process.

Britain's relative economic decline (relative to its rivals) can easily be illustrated with statistics, showing output of iron and steel (so crucial for weaponry) and the percentage of the world's manufacturing output produced by different countries.

Economic Output of the Great Powers, 1880 and, in brackets, 1913 (millions of tons)

	Iron and Steel	Percent of World Manufacturing Output	
Britain	4 (7.7)	22.9	(13.6)
France	1 (4.6)	7.8	(6.1)
Germany	1 (17.6)	8.5	(14.8)
Russia	0.5 (4.8)	7.6	(8.2)
USA	5 (31.8)	14.7	(32.0)

From the 1870s onwards, growth in industrial production was much slower in Britain than in several other countries. Given that there is a close connection between a country's economy and its foreign policy - stemming from the dependence of foreign policy upon military might, and of military might upon economic muscle - these trends were worrying to many Victorians. Paul Kennedy, in his immensely stimulating analysis of the 'the realities behind diplomacy', has insisted that this relative economic decline was 'the most crucial conditioning element' in the formulation of British foreign policy over the last century. Nevertheless, economic power did not translate itself automatically into foreign policy: also important were traditions, which led some countries to spend a greater portion of their resources on foreign policy than other states, as well as the decisions and strength of will of the policy-makers. Whereas many Britons were undoubtedly worried as the nineteenth century drew to its close, seeing the writing on the wall for British power in the world, others were more confident. After all, British economic power was declining slowly, and Britain remained, as late as 1914, one of the three strongest Powers in the world. Furthermore, diplomats aimed to avoid costly wars and to pursue a peaceful course in foreign policy, so that economic power would not be put to the test.

b) Public Opinion and the Electorate

Another factor relevant to foreign policy in this period was electoral reform. In 1832, with the Great Reform Act, a process began which substantially extended the vote. As a result of the Second Reform Act (1867) about one in three adult men could vote, while the Third Reform Act (1884-5) approximately doubled the percentage of those eligible to vote. Two-thirds of adult men could now elect their Members of

Parliament. Furthermore, legislation was passed to ensure that the ballot was secret and that corrupt practices were eliminated. Constituency boundaries were also reformed. Despite the fact that a third of men and all women were still unable to vote in national elections, Britain was undoubtedly becoming more democratic. At the same time, the Liberal and Conservative parties took on a 'modern' shape, each with local constituency parties and definite policies which they put before the electorate. In addition, the growth of education and of popular journalism contributed to the emergence of voters with an interest in, and knowledge of, foreign policy.

But what effects did these developments have? There were some who feared for the worst, believing that the extension of the franchise - and, more generally, the growth of mass 'public opinion' - would debase foreign policy. Instead of a small intelligent élite being left to decide what actions were necessary for the good of the nation, Britain's foreign policy would be prostituted in an attempt to buy votes from the credulous and ignorant masses. Instead of a broadly bipartisan foreign policy (supported by both parties), diplomacy might become a 'political football'. However, others believed that foreign policy had traditionally not served the national interest: it had been manipulated in the interests of a small clique and, therefore, could only gain by being subject to democratic pressures. Democratic thinkers believed that a foreign policy designed to foster the interests of the greatest number required participation by the many rather than the few. A third group, perhaps wisely uncertain about the future, simply waited to see what effects there would be.

4 Foreign Policy after 1865: an Overview

British policy-makers wanted to avoid war and to maintain British influence abroad. In short, they wanted to forestall change, perhaps realising that Britain was so wealthy and powerful that any change was likely to be for the worse. But, unfortunately for them, history would not stand still. The Ottoman Empire was rotting away as nationalism grew stronger; the United States of America was flexing its muscles in the western hemisphere; Japan was rising in the Far East; Russia was expanding along the Trans-Siberian Railway and, supported by France, seemed to pose momentous challenges; and Germany was growing economically stronger and becoming a dominant Power. There were problems in plenty for the British.

a) The Eastern Question

Britain's biggest commitment after 1865 was the guarantee to Turkey provided at the Congress of Paris. This served to embroil several governments in the problems of the Near East, especially when it became apparent that successive Sultans had no intentions of reforming their rule over Christian subjects in the Balkans. Crisis came in the late 1870s when the flamboyant Conservative Benjamin Disraeli was Prime Minister. In 1875 the Balkan provinces of Bosnia and Herzegovina rebelled against Ottoman rule, sparking off a warning from the Great Powers for Turkey to set its empire in order. However, Disraeli departed from this Great Power unanimity, pledging support for the Sultan and even sending ships to the Dardanelles. Disraeli was not merely adhering to pledges undertaken at the Congress of Paris, he was seeking prestige for himself and Britain. No other figure in the period 1865-1914 sought 'greatness' as consistently - and many said recklessly - as Disraeli.

In 1876, when further Balkan provinces rebelled, Disraeli found himself at odds with British public opinion. Turkish forces massacred Bulgarians, producing the greatest outburst from the public in the whole of the 1865-1914 period. To make matters worse for Disraeli, it was orchestrated by his hated rival, the Liberal William Gladstone. Disraeli's support for the Turks nearly led him into war on the side of Turkey when Russia took up arms in 1877, inflicting a major defeat on the Sultan. Britain wished to keep Russia away from the Straits, from which it might menace the route to India via the Suez Canal (opened in 1869), and also away from Constantinople, from where it could have access overland to India. The issue was temporarily settled in 1878 at the Congress of Berlin, when the German Chancellor, Bismarck, acted as mediator. Disraeli's popularity was now fully restored, and he boasted that he had brought back 'peace with honour'. By this settlement, Turkey lost some territory in the Balkans but not as much as the Russians had insisted upon after the war. Britain now guaranteed only Turkey-in-Asia, a less onerous commitment. In fact, Britain was ceasing to concern itself so much with the Ottoman Empire, realising that it was possible to protect the sea route to India from Mediterranean bases. Certainly Gladstone, in office after the 1880 election, had no intention of supporting the 'unspeakable Turk'. In the period 1908-14, when there were further troubles in the Balkans, Britain was not greatly involved, having ceased to recognise the area as one of vital importance to her own interests.

b) Gladstone and the Concert of Europe

Gladstone did not seek prestige: instead he aimed to use moral authority, and the Concert of Europe, to safeguard Britain's position and to solve European problems. He was undoubtedly much more peaceful, and much more of a genuine internationalist, than Disraeli, and the two men certainly looked upon themselves as having nothing in common with each other. Yet, rhetoric aside, there are similarities in their foreign policies. Disraeli stood for imperial greatness, and in 1876 he made Queen Victoria 'Empress of India', but it was Gladstone who, in 1882, authorised the invasion of Egypt. He did this with extreme reluctance, after local riots threatened not only British investments but the security of the Suez Canal. He had no intention of staying in Egypt, and yet his government could find no way of leaving. In effect, another colony had been added to the British Empire. In addition, Gladstone was unable to prevent the 'Scramble for Africa', which marked the 1880s and 1890s. The active search by rival countries for colonies meant that Britain could no longer rely on informal economic dominance: instead the Union Jack had to be raised. When he fell from office in 1885 he had failed to revive the Concert of Europe and his foreign policy seemed in tatters.

Most important of all, Gladstone's invasion of Egypt drove a wedge between Britain and France. Egypt had in fact been a sphere of French influence for some time, and it was the French who suggested the invasion, before backing out at the last moment. Anglo-French relations were then poor for the rest of the century. Mutual competition during the partition of Africa also produced a good deal of friction, especially during the Fashoda incident, on the Nile, in 1898. A war between the two countries seemed possible, but the French were too fearful of their German neighbours to push issues to extremes with Britain.

c) The End of 'Splendid Isolation'

Relations with France were bad in this period, but it was Russia that was identified as the major potential enemy in the second half of the nineteenth century. In particular, Russian designs upon India were constantly suspected. Disraeli almost went to war with Russia in 1877-8, and so did Gladstone in 1885. Relations were little better later in the century, when rivalry in China was added to the list of Anglo-Russian disagreements. Indeed it was a growth in the Russian fleet which produced a brief naval race with Britain. By 1894 the Russians had concluded an alliance with France, and British vessels in the Far East were consequently out-numbered, triggering an alliance between Britain and Japan in 1902.

The period between 1885 and 1902, when Lord Salisbury dominated British foreign policy, is often considered to be a time of 'splendid isolation'. In fact, this term is misleading: Salisbury did not want isolation, which he considered dangerous, but he did wish to avoid entangling alliances. Hence the alliance with Japan marks a retreat from traditions. It coincided with the ending of the Boer War, between Britain and the Dutch settlers in South Africa, a conflict which showed the dangers of British isolation. In addition, Britain and France settled their colonial differences in 1904 with the signing of the *Entente Cordiale* ('friendly understanding'), and in 1907 British quarrels with Russia in Afghanistan and Persia were settled, producing the Anglo-Russian

Entente. Consequently, some historians talk about a 'revolution' in British foreign policy in 1902-7. Certainly there was a major change. British fears of Russia still existed, and there was continuing friction over the next few years. But relations were now better than for some time. British policy-makers, anxious to avoid expensive war, were doing their best to remain on good terms with their European neighbours.

d) Anglo-German Antagonism

The most important of the European Powers after 1871 was Germany. At first there were considerable British fears that this new nation-state, which had just defeated France and imposed a tough peace settlement and whose economy began to grow so rapidly, might disrupt the balance of power in Europe. But there was little cause for alarm in the 1870s and 1880s. Chancellor Bismarck took a leading role in European affairs, but it was a peaceful role, as in the Congress of Berlin. Many Britons disliked the alliances he forged (especially since their terms were secret), but most grudgingly respected his expertise. He managed to keep France isolated, so that the French would be unable to wage a war of revenge, and he formed a link between Austria and Russia, two Powers with opposing interests in the Balkans. Above all, he made no move to challenge the supremacy of the Royal Navy at sea.

After his fall, in 1890, German policy was much more erratic. Good relations between Britain and Germany still seemed possible, and indeed at several points, especially in 1901, an Anglo-German alliance, or at least an entente, was on the cards. But increasingly relations deteriorated. Wilhelm II (Kaiser from 1888 to 1918), himself half-British, seemed to alienate the British at every possible opportunity. Above all, he began to build a much larger German navy, which the British thought was targeted at them. Soon an expensive naval race began, souring relations between the two states, and in 1905 and 1911 he precipitated crises in Morocco which drove the British and the French closer together. After 1905 the Entente with France began to take on more and more the qualities of an alliance: there were even secret military talks between British and French generals, and Britain undertook informal responsibility for defending part of the French coastline.

e) Outbreak of the First World War

By 1912 the Germans decided to focus on their army rather than their navy. After the naval race, an important arms race began. In this, however, Britain was less involved. The focus of international attention shifted once again to the Balkans, no longer a focus of British interest. There were localised wars in 1912 and 1913, during which Britain's role was limited to that of mediation by the Foreign Secretary, Sir Edward Grey, who sought to revive the Concert of Europe. However, another crisis flared up in the summer of 1914, this time between Serbia and Austria, and for once it was not localised. When Germany decided to back up its ally Austria, in the knowledge that it might well lead to war against Serbia's ally Russia and Russia's ally France, many thought there was an obligation on Britain to join on the side of its Entente partners. Moral obligations there may have been, but there was no legal requirement, and the Liberal cabinet debated the issue several times in the first days of August. Britain declared war, amidst considerable popular rejoicing, when Germany violated Belgium neutrality, which the British had guaranteed the previous century. Probably the main reason for entry was to stop Germany dominating the whole continent and thus destroying the balance of power and menacing Britain's own security.

In 1914 a British Expeditionary Force was sent to France. It was widely expected that the conflict would all be over by Christmas. In fact it ended in November - but November 1918 not 1914. Britain had entered the Great War, as contemporaries called it. It was the most destructive war of attrition in the history of the world. British politicians had indulged in several wars in the period 1865-1914, but these had been colonial conflicts, most no more than skirmishes in which superior weaponry made short work of their enemies. Even the Boer War of 1899-1902 had entailed only limited commitments. Greater conflicts had been avoided, even at the cost of losing face in contests with the United States of America. But now a 'total war' had begun. Not only are its origins one of the most widely and hotly debated issues in historical study, but its consequences were to be immensely significant. The War tested the might of Great Britain, including her economy, to the full. After it, neither Britain nor its foreign policy could be the same again.

Making notes on 'Introduction: Britain and the European Powers'

You will not need to make full notes on this chapter, which is designed to introduce several key themes, provide some background information on foreign policy before 1865 and provide a brief 'mental map' of the period up to 1914. It is important to grasp the essence of the 'Eastern Question' and the fact of Britain's relative economic decline between 1865 and 1914. The study diagram will familiarise you with some of the main events and trends of foreign policy in this period.

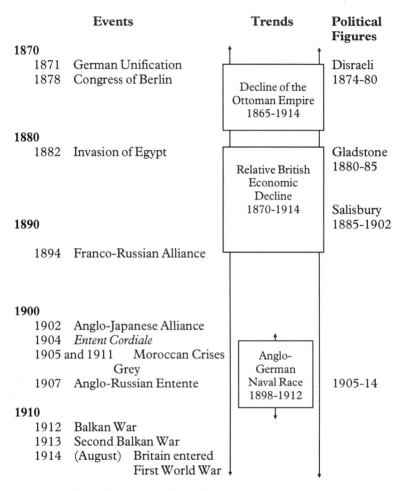

Events	Trends	Political Figures
1870		
1871 German Unification	Decline of the Ottoman Empire 1865-1914	Disraeli 1874-80
1878 Congress of Berlin		
1880		
1882 Invasion of Egypt	Relative British Economic Decline 1870-1914	Gladstone 1880-85
1890		Salisbury 1885-1902
1894 Franco-Russian Alliance		
1900		
1902 Anglo-Japanese Alliance		
1904 *Entent Cordiale*	Anglo-German Naval Race 1898-1912	1905-14
1905 and 1911 Moroccan Crises		
Grey		
1907 Anglo-Russian Entente		
1910		
1912 Balkan War		
1913 Second Balkan War		
1914 (August) Britain entered First World War		

Summary - Introduction: Britain and the European Powers

CHAPTER 2

Disraeli and Foreign Policy, 1865-80

Benjamin Disraeli (1804-81), the flamboyant son of a Jewish author, was the odd man out in British politics in the nineteenth century. His background was unique: he was not an aristocrat or landowner, had not been to public school, was a Christian only by conversion and was considered by many to be a cynical and unprincipled adventurer. Few believed that this 'foreigner' would pursue a traditional foreign policy. Yet in 1874-80, perhaps as the culmination of a lifelong battle to be accepted, he aspired to emulate Palmerston by ruthlessly furthering what he saw as Britain's national interests. The results of his actions are remarkably controversial. He can be seen as the most successful exponent of British foreign policy or as its most abysmal failure.

1 Foreign Policy from 1865-74

The period 1865-74 has been called one of 'suspended animation' in British diplomacy. Britain's policy, said the Foreign Secretary in 1866, was 'determined inaction ... the policy of not meddling'. In particular Britain seemed uninterested in Europe. Italy had been substantially unified by 1861, without British interference; and similarly Germany was unified without major British reaction. Two wars facilitated this unification: Britain remained neutral in the Austro-Prussian war of 1866 - the French ambassador commenting that 'England is simply a spectator of events' - and also in the Franco-Prussian war of 1871, which led to the final unification of Germany. Some Britons were uneasy at Bismarck's victory, which they thought (correctly, as it turned out) might herald the emergence of an overmighty Germany in the future, but most were relieved that the French had not won. Britain's greatest rival, France, would no longer be able to cause problems. As for Germany, it lacked a strong navy and an overseas empire and so was hardly likely to cause trouble for Britain. In the 1870s British spending on the navy was cut.

This was an era when free trade, as championed by Cobden and Bright, was in the ascendant. It was believed that free trade would lead to the eventual solution of all problems between states, binding them together and making war obsolete. There was therefore no need for an active foreign policy: instead, Britain should content herself with setting a civilised example to the world. Certainly, any search for 'prestige', it was widely believed, was an adolescent, unworthy goal for such a responsible, mature state. The best foreign policy was therefore the least foreign policy.

There were further reasons for this relative lack of interest in Europe.

In particular British trade tended to be with the wider world, including its own Empire, rather than the nearby continent. Disraeli pointed this out during his short-lived Conservative government of 1868:

1 The abstention of England from any unnecessary interference in the affairs of Europe is the consequence, not of her decline of power, but of her increased strength. England is no mere European Power; she is the metropolis of a great maritime empire, extending
5 to the boundaries of the farthest ocean ... She is really more an Asiatic power than a European ... But we are interested in the peace and prosperity of Europe, and I do not say that there may not be occasions in which it may be the duty of England to interfere in European wars.

There are signs in this speech that, in the mind of Disraeli, isolation from Europe might be short-lived. But at the end of 1868 the Liberals won power, and they had even less intention of European involvements.

William Ewart Gladstone (1809-98), Disraeli's great rival in Victorian politics, was Prime Minister from 1868 to 1874. In style he was the total opposite of Disraeli - puritanical and earnest where Disraeli was witty and frivolous. In addition, he was more concerned with morality, and with the preservation of peace. When, therefore, the Russians repudiated the Black Sea clauses of the Treaty of Paris (see page 6) in October 1870, Gladstone did no more than organise a conference in London which debated and then rubber-stamped their action. He also stood by passively while Germany was unified in 1871. It is true that he wished to issue a protest at Bismarck's annexation of the French provinces of Alsace and Lorraine, under the terms of the harsh Treaty of Frankfurt, but his cabinet vetoed even this mild measure. His only success was to insist that both the combatants respected the neutrality of neighbouring Belgium, the archetypal small nation whose integrity Liberals believed should be sacrosanct. Similarly he accepted international arbitration in 1872 to settle a dispute with the United States over the *Alabama*. This was built by Britons for the Southern States during the American Civil War, exploiting a loophole in Britain's neutrality law. It was designed to be merely a commercial ship, but it was used to sink a good many Northern vessels, and after the war the Americans demanded compensation. When a figure of £3.25 million was decided upon, Gladstone's government duly paid, even though the figure was widely thought to be excessive. Gladstone was hoping to inaugurate a new era of co-operation and responsibility in international affairs and wished to see the general acceptance of a morality which transcended national interests, even British ones. He believed that foreign policy should be built on solid ethical foundations. But to critics, his policy seemed weak and totally unworthy of a great country like Britain.

2 The Impact of Disraeli

The foremost of these critics, Disraeli, became Prime Minister himself in 1874. Aged seventy and in poor health, he lamented that power had come to him too late. Yet he immediately brought a new panache to foreign policy. On assuming office he wanted to do something - critics say anything - to cut a dash in foreign affairs. Not for him any Cobdenite passivity. Already, in 1873, he had protested against the formation of a Three Emperor's League (Dreikaiserbund) in Europe, consisting of Germany, Austria and Russia, describing it as an 'unnatural alliance' (largely because Britain had no part in it). Now, in 1875, he asserted Britain's claim to a voice in European affairs. A 'war scare' began: it was rumoured that Bismarck was about to invade France. The French then looked round for allies: Russia issued a protest to Berlin and so, seeing an ideal opportunity to drive a wedge between two members of the League, did Disraeli. British and Russian diplomats worked closely together, and there was even talk of a possible alliance. The immediate crisis was soon over - Bismarck protesting that he had never even contemplated war - but so too was Britain's isolation from European affairs.

Not that Disraeli confined his attentions to Europe. He was also interested in the wider world and was a self-proclaimed imperialist. Indeed in 1872 he had castigated the Liberals for trying to effect the 'disintegration of the Empire of England' and had insisted that the correct policy for Conservatives was 'the maintenance of the Empire'. It used to be argued that these views were sheer opportunism on Disraeli's part, but in fact they were sincerely held and had featured in his speeches for some time. He had once spoken of the colonies as 'millstones around our neck', but that had been no more than momentary irritation. Admittedly he did not, as Prime Minister, take any real interest in individual colonies, but he did regard the Empire as a vital symbol of British greatness in the world.

In 1875 he showed great boldness and flair in Egypt, an outpost of the Ottoman Empire. In the 1860s the ruler (Khedive) of Egypt had tried, with some success, to develop the country with foreign loans; but his debts began to mount, and soon repayments were totalling two-thirds of his annual income. To stave off bankruptcy, therefore, he offered 44 per cent of the shares in the Suez Canal Company for sale. The Canal was vital for British shipping: indeed ever since it had been completed by the French in 1869, the main route to India, and also Australasia, had been via the Mediterranean and the Suez Canal, a much shorter and consequently more economical route than around the Cape, in southern Africa. Egypt was the key to this short-cut to India, and therefore Disraeli, seeing his opportunity in 1875, stepped in, borrowing £4 million from the Rothschilds because parliament was not sitting and so could not immediately vote the money. Britain now became the largest single shareholder in the canal. Disraeli had not managed to buy a controlling interest in it - and he certainly won no friends in Paris - but he had prevented French domination. His financial coup heightened British prestige, as well as proving a sound investment, the value of the shares increasing tenfold by 1914. Another eye-catching initiative came in 1876 when Disraeli arranged for Queen Victoria to become 'Empress of India'. The possibility of such a title had been talked about ever since the British government had taken over the formal administration of India from the East India Company at the end of the 1850s. Now Disraeli gave the Queen the position she coveted. Britain's *imperial* monarch was no whit inferior to the Emperors of Germany, Russia and Austria. The change trumpeted to the world that Britain was no isolationist state: she was a great and triumphant Empire, and everyone should know it.

3 Disraeli and the Eastern Question, 1875-6

Disraeli became fully involved with Europe because of the continuing problems of the Ottoman Empire (see page 4 for the basis of the Eastern Question). This issue dominated British politics in 1875-8 and strained Disraeli's diplomatic ingenuity to the uttermost. The Eastern Question brought Britain to within an ace of war with Russia; it resulted at one stage in an unpopularity which seemed likely to unseat the Conservative leader; but - in the end - it crowned him with success at the Congress of Berlin. Not surprisingly, historians have written remarkably divergent interpretations of his policies and their effects in this area.

Trouble flared up in the Balkans in 1875, when the Ottoman (Turkish) Sultan, Abdul Aziz, reneged on his debts. His expenditure had exceeded his income ever since the Crimean War, and he regularly had to increase taxes to pay mounting bills. But now his credit ran out and the regime was bankrupt. Could the Ottoman Empire ('the Sick Man of Europe') finally be about to die? Certainly there seemed little life left in the Empire. Aziz's rule had been marked by maladministration, as well as heavy taxation, while the Sultan himself lived in a dream-world, even ennobling poultry in his royal apartments. To make matters worse, two Balkan provinces, Bosnia and Herzegovina, peopled mainly by Christians and resentful at punitive taxes and rule by Muslim landowners, rose up against their Ottoman (mis)rulers in December 1875. At this point the League of Three Emperors - in a Note named after the Austrian Foreign Secretary Andrassy - urged the Turks to implement a programme of reforms, so that further rebellions might be avoided. Turkish decline in the Balkans was an issue that might divide two members of the League, Austria and Russia, both of whom had vital interests in the area (see page 4). But for the time being, under Bismarck's watchful gaze, they were acting in concert.

Disraeli himself was in two minds how to react. On the one hand, he disapproved of the Note. He wished to bolster Turkey in the Balkans as a bulwark against Russian expansion, not to allow Russia, and its allies, greater influence. To his mind, there were good reasons to continue with this traditional British policy: it would prevent Russia becoming a Mediterranean power which might menace the route to India via the Suez canal, and, secondly, it would keep the Russians out of Constantinople, whence they might be able to make an overland attack on India via Afghanistan. India was thus central to his imperial thinking, and he was determined to protect this 'greatest jewel' in the British imperial crown. He also wanted to protect large British investments in the Ottoman Empire. In addition, he clearly disliked the fact that Britain had not been consulted by the League, whose very existence he resented. On the other hand, he did not feel committed to preserving Turkish rule at all costs and was aware that most Britons felt profoundly uneasy about propping up Turkish (and therefore Muslim) rule over Christians in the Balkans. There is even evidence that he contemplated changing British policy completely by throwing over the Turks and protecting British interest in the Balkans in alliance with Austria or with newly emerging independent states. Perhaps there might even be an Anglo-Russian alliance. This was a period when policy in the Near East was relatively fluid. Bismarck even suggested partitioning the Turkish Empire, with the province of Egypt being Britain's share. However, traditional fears of Russian expansion were strong and uncertainties at the consequences of Turkish partition were great. For the moment the British government decided to do little, merely acquiescing passively in the initiative of the League. In fact, this unusual inactivity was probably the result not so much of Disraeli, an instinctive activist, as of his Foreign Secretary, Lord Derby, a man of a very different stamp, instinctively passive and cautious and much influenced by Cobdenism.

Yet the insurrection in the Balkans dragged on, resulting in the deaths of several European consuls, and in May 1876 the Three Emperors' League issued a much stronger warning, known as the Berlin Memorandum. The Sultan was to settle his problems in the Balkans or face the consequences. France and Italy lent their support to this threat, especially since it seemed possible that not only Bosnia and Herzegovina but other Balkan provinces, including Serbia, Montenegro and Bulgaria, would also rise up against their Muslim overlords, producing a major conflagration. Derby wished Britain to act in concert with the other Powers. Yet Disraeli virtually vetoed the Memorandum, offering the Turks his full diplomatic support and even sending British ships to Besika Bay, close to the Dardanelles, as Palmerston had once done. This provocative action seemed calculated to leave the Eastern Question unsolved, for the more Britain supported him, the less likely was the Sultan to put his house in order. Why, then, did Disraeli take this action? Privately he complained not of the contents of the Memorandum but of the fact that Britain had not been consulted at the outset: 'They are beginning to treat England as if we were Montenegro or Bosnia'. It seems likely, therefore, that he was motivated primarily by a wish to assert British prestige and, if possible, to wreck the League. At once Disraeli became immensely popular with portions of the British population. He was asserting Britain's power in the world and standing up to the Europeans, showing independence and initiative. The Prime Minister remarked that 'something like the old days of our authority' had returned. Queen Victoria approved his action by making him Earl of Beaconsfield. But to others, including Derby and members of his own cabinet, he was acting unreasonably: he had isolated Britain and was risking another Crimean War, and all this for the Turks, allies who were unworthy of British support.

Britain did not become embroiled in war, but this was partly due to luck - a revolution in Constantinople. Disraeli could take no credit for this, since his support for Turkey was a conservative force, propping up the Sultan and dissuading him of the need for reform. Yet in 1876 Abdul Aziz was deposed in favour of his son, Prince Murad (a weak-minded youth much addicted to champagne laced with brandy), who in the same year gave way to his half-brother Abdul Hamid. Finally, observers believed, an efficient and progressive regime had emerged. This Sultan accepted a new constitution, and the first ever Ottoman parliament soon met. The Berlin Memorandum was thus rendered redundant and so was withdrawn. Britain, it seemed, had been saved from the consequences of its policy of propping up Turkey.

Yet, in reality, the problems in the Balkans had not been solved; and since the Great Powers took no action against the Ottoman Empire, the Balkan states decided to do so themselves. In June 1876 Serbia and Montenegro declared war on the Turks, and Bulgarian patriots also tried to overthrow Turkish rule. Disraeli's popularity was to vanish overnight.

4 The 'Bulgarian Horrors'

In June 1876 the Sultan's army massacred around 12,000 Bulgarian Christians. Babies were speared by Turkish soldiers, and men and women impaled on posts. Over 70 villages were destroyed, together with 200 schools and 10 monasteries. These atrocities received enormous publicity in Britain. The story broke in the *Daily News,* where an exaggerated figure of around 25,000 deaths - of men, women and children - was reported, together with gory details of torture, rape and sodomy. There followed a tremendous outcry of moral indignation from the British public. Hundreds of meetings were held throughout the country denouncing the government's pro-Turkish policy. When, during a performance of *Othello* in Liverpool, the phrase 'The Turks are drowned' was recited, the audience rose up enthusiastically and interrupted the performance for some time with their cheering. A leading historian of the day judged that Britain was in danger of drifting into war 'on the side of the devil and in the cause of Hell', fighting against human freedom; and there were calls, instead, for a policy of national and Christian emancipation in the Balkan provinces. It was, perhaps, the greatest storm over foreign policy in British history. Surely no one would defend 'the Turk', stereotyped by Gladstone as 'the one great anti-human specimen of humanity'.

Gladstone had resigned the leadership of the Liberal Party after its defeat at the 1874 election, though retaining his seat in the Commons. He had lost faith in the electorate. But in 1876, sensing the new mood of moral outrage among the public, he returned to the political fray. He had always believed that politics should be a moral crusade. Now, some said rather belatedly, he placed himself at the head of the opposition to Disraeli's foreign policy. As the British expert on the Bulgarian Horrors, Richard Shannon, has written: this episode was 'less a case of Gladstone exciting popular passion than of popular passion exciting Gladstone'. In September he published *Bulgarian Horrors and the Question of the East,* written in three days while he was in bed with lumbago. This pamphlet soon sold 200,000 copies. It was full of fiery rhetoric. The Turks, in indulging their 'abominable and bestial lusts', had enacted scenes 'at which Hell itself might almost blush'. He argued that the British government,

1 which has been working in one direction, shall work in the other, and shall apply all its vigour to concur with other states of Europe in obtaining the extinction of the Turkish executive power in Bulgaria. Let the Turks now carry away their abuses in the only 5 possible manner, namely by carrying off themselves ... One and all, bag and baggage, shall, I hope, clear out from the province they have desolated and profaned.

Gladstone's policy was less radical than, at first sight, it appeared: he was insisting that the Turks should leave only Bulgaria, not the whole of the Balkans. Nevertheless, Britain's foreign policy in the Near East had become the central political issue of the day, and the country became sharply divided on the atrocity issue.

Disraeli wrote privately that, of all the horrors, Gladstone's pamphlet was 'perhaps the greatest'. Publicly, he might have been expected to be more diplomatic, but not so. When the story first broke, he insisted that the cruelties were 'to a large extent inventions', and he shrugged them aside as 'coffee-house babble'. To the House of Commons, in his last speech before entering the Lords as Beaconsfield, he insisted that Orientals 'seldom resort to torture but generally terminate their connexion with culprits in a more expeditious manner'. This was an example of Disraeli's loquacious style, but many people thought he was making a joke - in profoundly bad taste. The truth of the matter is that,

NEUTRALITY UNDER DIFFICULTIES.

Dizzy. "BULGARIAN ATROCITIES! I ·CAN'T FIND THEM IN THE ' OFFICIAL REPORTS'!!!"

Neutrality Under Difficulties, Punch, *5 August 1876*

initially, Disraeli had been misinformed: he was told by the pro-Turkish ambassador in Constantinople, Sir Henry Elliot, that there was little truth in the stories, whereas in fact they did contain much accurate information. But then he stubbornly refused to budge, and in fact he never once condemned the massacre. Indeed he seemed unperturbed by the matter, (see the cartoon from *Punch* on page 21). He would not admit that his old rival, Gladstone, had justice on his side. A dangerous inflexibility had crept into Disraeli's attitude. Gladstone said he and the Liberals stood for 'the higher moral law', whereas Disraeli insisted that the Conservatives would always stand for the 'permanent and abiding interests of England'. But could it really be in Britain's interests, people asked, to support the 'unspeakable Turk'?

Disraeli's foreign policy in the summer of 1876 was, to put it bluntly, in a mess. He wanted to resist Russian domination in the Balkans by propping up Turkey, and he wanted the sort of firm policy which would prove popular at home. But these aims were simply incompatible: it was impossible to gain popularity by being pro-Turk. Indeed, it soon became clear that the new Sultan was one of the worst tyrants in Turkish history. Abdul Hamid dismissed the new Ottoman parliament, which was never recalled, and was revealed as reactionary (reasserting Muslim values) and as paranoid (sheltering behind a huge spy network and shooting at officials and gardeners in his palace at will). Such was Britain's ally. Gladstone called Abdul Hamid's mind 'a bottomless pit of fraud and falsehood'. Disraeli himself was quite prepared to sup with the devil, but the British population simply would not accept overtly pro-Turkish actions at this time. Public opinion had effectively paralysed his foreign policy. All he could do, therefore, since he was unwilling to admit mistakes and reverse policy, was to mark time until, as he put it, 'the people of England ... have quite recovered their senses'. In fact, he had not long to wait.

5 The Russo-Turkish War

Individual Russians flocked to join their fellow Slavs and Orthodox Christians in the war against Turkey, Tolstoy remarking in his novel *Anna Karenina* that the heroism of the Serbians 'begot in the whole Russian people a longing to help their brothers not in word but in deed'. The Tsar, Alexander II, proclaimed official Russian neutrality, but there were tremendous pressures on him from the press and clergy to declare war, especially when the Turks emerged victorious. Panslav advisers assured him that, after the Bulgarian agitation in Britain, Disraeli's government would be unable to respond, and therefore in November 1876 Tsar Alexander made an aggressive speech and looked likely to declare war. From this time onwards there were signs that traditional anti-Russian feelings were beginning to increase in Britain. It seemed at least possible that, if the trend continued, anti-Turkish feelings might eventually be smothered by the growth of anti-Russian sentiments.

Lord Derby moved quickly to calm the situation. In November 1876 he seized the initiative from his Prime Minister by calling a conference at Constantinople to settle problems peacefully and prevent Great Power conflict. Britain was represented by Lord Salisbury, the Secretary of State for India, who was well known for being critical of existing foreign policy. At the conference, Salisbury was all for joining with the other Powers in forcing concessions from the Turks. Disraeli was indignant, writing privately that Salisbury did not seem to realise that 'his principal object ... is to keep the Russians out of Turkey, not to create an ideal existence for Turkish Christians', but it seemed that the Prime Minister would have to give way on the direction of foreign policy. However, he still had a trick or two up his sleeve. When Salisbury asked for the

Map of the Balkans at the time of the Russo-Turkish War

removal of ambassador Elliot, who was preventing agreement in Constantinople, Disraeli turned down the request; and the Sultan was satisfied that he could count on the British Prime Minister's support. Abdul Hamid therefore resisted all pressure for reform, including suggestions for the creation of an autonomous Bulgarian state in the Balkans. The conference then broke up in disarray.

Disraeli was undoubtedly playing a dangerous game, and many have criticised him. Robert Blake, his generally sympathetic biographer, has judged that he had now lost his former flexibility: 'The more Turcophobe Gladstone became, the more Russophobe was Disraeli'. Certainly the failure of negotiations gave the Tsar little choice, and in April 1877 he lost patience and declared war on Turkey. In consequence, an Anglo-Russian war looked a distinct possibility.

Would Britain join the war? There were divided counsels. Queen Victoria was all for Britain entering. To her mind the issue was quite clear: 'it is a question of Russian or British supremacy in the world'. On the other hand, the Foreign Secretary wanted to avoid war. Derby believed that his Prime Minister was 'not drifting but rushing into war', and all for an intangible 'prestige'. He wrote, almost incredulously, that Disraeli 'would think it (quite sincerely) in the interests of the country to spend 200 millions on a war if the result was to make foreign states think more highly of us'. However, there is considerable doubt as to whether Disraeli really wanted war. Certainly he saw the need to threaten hostilities, in order to keep Russia out of Constantinople, but he may well have hoped that the threat would be sufficient. The most he advocated was the seizure of the Dardanelles, which would put Britain in a good position if it came to war, a brinkmanship Derby considered too provocative. The breach between Disraeli and Derby was now almost complete, and the Foreign Secretary was on the verge of resignation for several months. He even went so far as to undermine his leader by leaking secrets to Shuvalov, the Russian ambassador in London, to show that the whole cabinet was not bent on confrontation. Disraeli was fully aware of this division: he even judged, at one point, that the twelve men in his cabinet advocated, between them, seven different policies! Because of this disunity, and because of his uncertainty about public opinion, he decided against positively warlike actions. He also found it impossible to negotiate joint action with Austria (whose neutrality had been secured by a Russian promise of the cession of Bosnia and Herzegovina once the war had been won). Once again, therefore, he allowed policy to drift.

Matters came to a head at the start of 1878. Plevna (see the map on page 23) had fallen to the Russians after a long siege, and now the Turks asked for British help. Disraeli was adamant that something had to be done. After all, the Russians were occupying Adrianople, and so were within easy reach of the greatest prize of all, the Turkish capital of Constantinople. Queen Victoria felt so strongly on the matter that she threatened to abdicate unless strong action were taken. ('Oh, if the Queen were a man,' she wrote, 'she would like to go and give those Russians, whose word one cannot believe, such a beating.') Public opinion also now seemed to favour action. The Turks' defence of Plevna had been unsuccessful but heroic, and the Bulgarian Horrors were quickly forgotten: a second pamphlet by Gladstone on this theme sold a mere 7,000 copies, and a London mob showed its feelings by breaking the windows of his house. The public was not exactly pro-Turkish but at least anti-Turkish feeling had subsided, and there seemed no doubt that strong anti-Russian sentiment existed. A famous music hall song expressed the growing anti-Russian feeling:

1 The Dogs of War are loose, and the rugged Russian Bear,
  Full bent on blood and robbery, has crawled out of his lair,
  It seems a thrashing now and then will never help to tame
  That brute, and so he's bent upon the same old game.
5 The Lion did his best to find him some excuse
  To crawl back to his den again; all efforts were no use.
  He hungered for his victim, he's pleased when blood is shed,
  But let us hope his crimes may recoil on his own head.

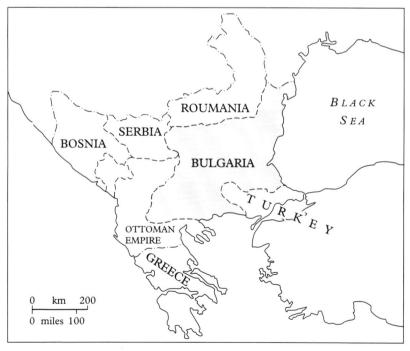

Map of the 'Big Bulgaria' of the Treaty of San Stefano

We don't want to fight, but by Jingo! if we do
10 We've got the ships, we've got the men,
We've got the money too.
We've fought the Bear before, and while we're Britons true,
The Russians shall not have Constantinople.

These lyrics, which gave the word 'jingoism' to the language, are evidence of a more aggressive nationalism in Britain; but before any decisive action was taken, the Turks had sued for peace and Count Ignatiev, the Panslav Russian minister in Constantinople, had imposed the Treaty of San Stefano (see the map on page 25). This represented a great victory for the Russians, who achieved almost all they wanted. The treaty virtually destroyed Turkey-in-Europe. It confirmed the independence of Serbia and Montenegro (both of which now became larger) and of Romania; it ordered Turkey to pay a large indemnity; and, most controversially of all, it created an independent 'Big Bulgaria', which would absorb Macedonia and stretch from the Black Sea to the Aegean.

To most Britons the settlement was unacceptably harsh, and yet again war was contemplated. Bulgaria might be independent of Turkey, but it was expected to be far from independent of Russia. Indeed it was widely seen as merely a Russian satellite. Certainly it was to be administered and garrisoned by Russia for an initial period of two years, and so Russia would gain access to the Mediterranean. Disraeli immediately called up the army reserve and sent 7,000 troops from India to Malta, Britain's Mediterranean colony, while at the same time laying secret plans to seize Cyprus, provocative moves which finally led Derby to resign. He was replaced by Lord Salisbury.

The new man had not seen eye-to-eye with Disraeli in the past, and he told the Prime Minister that he did not believe 'in the possibility of setting the Turkish Government on its legs again, as a genuine reliable Power'. He thought, instead, that Britain should defend only Turkey-in-Asia, thus safeguarding the route to India. There was, therefore, a possibility of continued strife within the Conservative cabinet. But Salisbury's appointment was a good one nevertheless. He was a firmer negotiator than Derby and an altogether stronger figure. San Stefano increased his fear of the Russians, so that it eclipsed his genuine distaste for the Turks. Therefore he was able to cooperate much more closely with Disraeli than his predecessor had done. A new clarity was soon imposed on British foreign policy.

Britain was in a strong position after the treaty of San Stefano. There were several reasons for this. Russia was exhausted by the war with Turkey and was in no position to carry on fighting, and there were influential Russians who themselves disliked the treaty. Shuvalov, for instance, called it 'the greatest act of stupidity that we could have committed'. Furthermore, Austria was aggrieved. Russian control of an enlarged Bulgaria seemed to menace Austrian interests as well as British, and moreover Austria had not, as promised, received Bosnia and Herzegovina from the settlement. The Austrians therefore hotly complained. The League of Three Emperors, in consequence, finally came to an end, much to Disraeli's delight. Nor would he have to go to war to reverse San Stefano, for Austria demanded a conference to settle the issue, and Bismarck, acting as 'honest broker', called one in Berlin. The Russians had little choice but to attend, and it seemed certain that they would bow before combined Anglo-Austrian-German pressure.

6 The Congress of Berlin

a) The Agreements

The Congress was a great set-piece of diplomacy, and both Disraeli and Salisbury attended for Britain. But most issues had been settled before the delegates assembled, especially by Salisbury and Shuvalov in London, with Bismarck lending his authority to their behind-the-scenes negotiations. Disraeli's health was poor in Berlin, and indeed Salisbury described him as having only 'the dimmest idea of what is going on' and of understanding 'everything sideways', but all that remained was to finalise arrangements and announce the results with a blaze of publicity.

There were three basic agreements (see the map on page 28):

i) On the central issue of Bulgaria there was a compromise: it was divided into three. A Bulgarian state was set up, but it was to be autonomous, rather than completely independent of Turkey, and it was to be much smaller than in the treaty of San Stefano. It was to lose not only Macedonia, which was returned to Turkey as an integral province, but also the area that had briefly been southern Bulgaria. This was to become a semi-autonomous province within the Turkish empire (but with a Christian governor) known as Eastern Roumelia. Possession of Eastern Roumelia would allow the Turks to garrison the line of the Balkan mountains and to control the all-important mountain passes, and so, the British hoped, provide an effective barrier to Russian expansion. Disraeli insisted that he would go to war rather than compromise on these issues, and he had his way despite last-minute Russian objections. Thus Russian influence was pushed further away from Constantinople and the Mediterranean. On the other hand, Disraeli did not have things all his way. In 1876 he had set his face against the loss of any Turkish territory in the Balkans and had seemed willing to go to war rather than see the emergence of a Bulgaria of any size. Now he was prepared to accept Bulgarian self-government, much as Gladstone had advocated. Though he never admitted it, Disraeli had moderated his position.

ii) Austria-Hungary was to administer the Ottoman provinces of Bosnia and Herzegovina, while other areas in the Balkans, including Serbia, Romania and Montenegro, were to be recognised as independent of Turkey. Nevertheless, Turkey-in-Europe re-emerged: it occupied 60,000 square miles and included six million people. Critics believed it was monstrous that so many Christians had been returned to Ottoman rule, though of course Disraeli was pleased.

iii) Russia recovered the Bessarabian territory it had lost after the Crimean War and also received the port of Batum on the eastern coast of the Black Sea from Turkey. As compensation, it was agreed that Britain should annex the Ottoman island of Cyprus (described by Disraeli as 'the key to Asia'): from here Britain would be able to check any Russian advance. The British also issued a unilateral declaration, insisting that they had the right to force a passage through the Straits in order to safeguard Constantinople. Finally, Disraeli secured a promise that Turkey would reform its administration and treat its Christian subjects

Map of Congress of Berlin Settlement

better, but henceforth, as Salisbury advised, Britain would guarantee only Turkey-in-Asia.

The settlement was a classic compromise, with something for everyone - Austria, Russia, Turkey and Britain. The British public was pleased with the settlement, and Disraeli (or Beaconsfield, as he now was) was at the height of his popularity. He insisted that he had brought back 'peace with honour', and, ignoring the fact that in reality Berlin was now the diplomatic capital of the continent, he wrote to the Queen that she was 'the arbitress of Europe'. He told the House of Lords that the revision of San Stefano which he had achieved would have been satisfactory even at the cost of war, but that his victory had come about 'without shedding the blood of a single Englishman'. Britain had certainly emerged as a European Power of importance. Disraeli and the German Chancellor Bismarck had worked closely and harmoniously

'A Blaze of Triumph', Punch, *27 July 1878*

together (each respecting the other as an exponent of *realpolitik,* politics based upon practical realities not ethics), and they were the two outstanding figures at the Congress. Disraeli received the Order of the Garter on his return, and insisted that his Foreign Secretary, Salisbury, should be a recipient as well. Yet a cartoon from *Punch* indicated that Disraeli had been running great risks (see page 29). How much credit should he really receive?

b) Interpretations: Favourable

On the positive side, it can be said that Disraeli achieved all his major aims at Berlin. He had preserved some Balkan territory for Turkey, and so Turkey could be expected to act as a barrier to Russian expansion. Certainly Russia was kept out of Constantinople. He had also gained prestige for Britain (and for himself), together with a new possession, Cyprus, which was of strategic value in the eastern Mediterranean. He had avoided war, using only the threat of war to achieve his aims, and had thus forged a successful middle course between the doves and hawks in the country. Britain was now, once again, a power to be reckoned with in Europe, and the League of Three Emperors was at an end. Some historians have therefore insisted that Disraeli had succeeded brilliantly, despite opposition in his own cabinet and divisions in the country, and despite the fact that his own health was failing, so that he was not able to attend the final day's banquet. The Berlin settlement may not have been perfect, Disraeli's biographer Robert Blake has noted: but 'it was followed by almost as long a period of peace between the European great powers as the interval separating the Crimean War from the Congress of Vienna. As one of the two principal plenipotentiaries at Berlin Disraeli must share with Bismarck some part of the credit'. It should also be stressed that the treaty of San Stefano would have been unlikely to provide long-term security in the area. The Big Bulgaria would have contained too many non-Bulgars, and thus Bulgaria might have replaced Turkey as a resented foreign ruler to be overthrown by nationalist uprisings.

Richard Millman, who has written the most detailed account of the Eastern Question in 1875-8, has concluded that if Disraeli did not exactly bring back peace with honour, he certainly secured 'peace with prestige'. This 'bracing assertion of national strength and purpose' came after 'a period of fifteen years during which the policy and position of England were too often marked by self-effacement, embarrassment, and ignominy'. It was therefore 'welcome nectar after so long a drought'.

c) Interpretations: Unfavourable

However, Disraeli's participation in the Eastern Question has also been seen in a more jaundiced light. It is true that he preserved Turkey-in-Europe to some extent; but it is quite possible that more Turkish territory might have remained in the Balkans if Disraeli had supported the Berlin Memorandum of 1876, his blocking of which helped to precipitate the Russo-Turkish war. Instead, he had needlessly risked a war with Russia. Disraeli had boasted that Britain had no reason to fear war: 'Her Majesty has Fleets and Armies which are second to none'. Yet this was patently untrue, and the army was particularly weak, Britain being the only major power which had not introduced conscription. In the 1860s Bismarck had replied to the suggestion that British troops might intervene against him by saying that, if they did, 'We should send the police force to arrest them'; and at the end of the 1870s British forces were no more formidable. A war against Russia, with no continental allies, would certainly have proved expensive and burdensome and might well have been catastrophic.

Only a large measure of luck prevented such a war: and if Derby had not been so adamantly against war, even luck might not have sufficed. The much-maligned Derby - whom contemporaries believed, without proof, to be drinking far too much - deserves more credit than he has ever received. At one time he stood alone against the whole cabinet in blocking anti-Russian moves which might have precipitated war. A colleague noted that Derby 'is so timid and irresolute that all the rest of the Cabinet cannot move him'. Some timidity, some irresolution!

Why did Disraeli risk war? To preserve the Indian empire from Russian encroachments, said his supporters, an entirely proper motive. But several commentators have found it hard to avoid the conclusion that his primary aim was not to safeguard India or to solve the Eastern Question but simply to bolster British prestige. A hard-headed (*realpolitik*) appraisal of British interests might well have led Disraeli to the conclusion that the Turkish cause in Europe was doomed, and that Britain should therefore have sought other means of protecting the routes to the East. Certainly Lord Salisbury believed that the old policy of protecting European Turkey was played-out and irrelevant. In 1877 Salisbury said that the 'commonest error in politics is sticking to the carcasses of dead policies'. The Balkans may have been an obsession with Disraeli, who would have achieved more diplomatically if his geography had been better. Salisbury commented wryly that larger-scale maps would have made all the difference to foreign policy. Disraeli once said - foolishly - that if the Russians were in Constantinople they would threaten the Suez Canal, forgetting that around 1,000 miles lay between them. Salisbury came to realise that liberated Slav nations in the Balkans would provide a more effective barrier to Russian expansion than Turkish rule, but Disraeli (whom Salisbury once called 'a mere political gamester') never shared this insight. Was he simply too old to rethink his basic assumptions?

The Berlin agreements may have brought Disraeli temporary

prestige, but the settlement soon fell apart. An Austro-German alliance was signed in 1879 and in 1881 another Three Emperors' League was formed, thus ending Anglo-Austrian co-operation in the Balkans and, once again, isolating Britain in Europe. Furthermore, the division of Bulgaria was ended in 1885, when it absorbed Eastern Roumelia. A further charge against Disraeli is that the new Bulgaria, rather than being a Russian pawn, soon showed anti-Russian attitudes: again Disraeli got it wrong. In addition, it must be noted that the Sultan's promises of reform were worth precisely nothing - and indeed there were to be further massacres of Christians - and that Cyprus proved useless as a naval base. Its possession also led to considerable troubles for Britain in the twentieth century. R.W. Seton-Watson, the author of a pioneering study on the Eastern Question and one of Disraeli's foremost critics, has judged that 'it is well for Disraeli that there are other fields in which his fame stands sure and unassailable: for his last great incursion into foreign policy was a failure'. In his view, and in that of other critics, the Berlin settlement did not ensure peace until 1914; on the contrary, it left so many unresolved problems that the Balkans fuelled tension in European affairs and eventually produced the First World War.

7 Imperial Troubles

Perhaps Disraeli should have called a general election as soon as he returned from Berlin. Certainly his popularity had declined markedly by 1880, when he did hold an election. Events in the British Empire tarnished his image significantly.

One area of strife was Afghanistan, a buffer state between British India and a Russia whose territory had expanded in the 1860s up to the Afghan borders. The Viceroy of India, Lord Lytton, felt vulnerable and argued that Britain ought to control Afghanistan in order to provide adequate security for India. The situation looked menacing when the Amir of Afghanistan received a mission from Russia in 1878; and Lytton, an impetuous man who was prone to ignoring instructions from London, decided to send his own agent, against the Amir's wishes. In fact the Tsar withdrew his mission, to avoid upsetting Anglo-Russian relations, but Lytton sent his men into Afghanistan nevertheless, triggering a successful invasion by the Indian army at the end of the year. The Amir fled and his son concluded a treaty which gave Britain control of his foreign policy. A British Resident was installed in the Afghan capital, Kabul. So far, so good: events had brought welcome prestige to Disraeli's government, even though politicians in Whitehall had little control over the actions of the 'men on the spot'. However, in September 1879 the Resident and his staff were killed by mutineers in the Afghan army, and war began again. It was still raging when the British general election was held the following year, thus providing fuel for Liberal critics of the government.

Further problems occurred in Southern Africa. What is today South Africa was, in the 1870s, occupied by two Dutch (or Boer) provinces (the Transvaal and the Orange Free State) which thought of themselves as being independent, two British colonies (Cape Colony and Natal) and a number of independent African kingdoms. Britain's ambitions in the area were conditioned by lack of revenue: the majority of Britons in the area were poor farmers, and customs revenues were limited. Indeed the area seemed likely to become of ever diminishing importance as the Suez Canal now took the great bulk of the trade to the east. All that Britain wanted, therefore, was stability, which it was thought could be achieved by a federation of the four provinces. But two problems stood in the way of federation: the menace posed by the Zulus and the unwillingness of the Boers to co-operate. In fact, the one helped to solve the other. In return for promising aid against the Zulus, Britain was able to annex the Transvaal in 1877, as a first step towards federation. Things seemed to be working out very nicely from the British government's point of view. On the other hand, it was not so easy to deal with the Zulu peoples. British troops were despatched to the area, though with orders that they should only be used defensively. Yet the High Commissioner in South Africa, Sir Bartle Frere, decided that the Zulus would have to be destroyed and so he deliberately provoked a war by presenting the Zulu chief with an ultimatum he could not accept. Disraeli believed privately that Frere ought to be impeached, but events soon necessitated the sending of reinforcements. In particular the loss of almost 1,000 British soldiers when their camp was attacked at Isandhlwana, generally regarded as the most humiliating British defeat in Africa, made it imperative that a decisive victory be won. Vengeance had to be exacted. The ensuing full-scale war against the Zulus did indeed end in victory, but only after several months' hard fighting which proved costly in terms of lives (2,400 Britons, and far more Africans, killed) and money (over £5 million).

Disraeli had not wished for this confrontation, any more than for that in Afghanistan: his government merely reacted to events, rather than initiating them. His contribution to the expansion of empire had thus been largely negative - he simply failed to restrain the 'men on the spot'. Perhaps he might have disciplined these 'agents' in the Empire more if the Queen had supported them less. Perhaps also he would have had less trouble if he had been a better judge of character: after all, he himself had chosen Lytton as Viceroy. It is also possible that his speeches, which were full of imperial rhetoric, encouraged Britons on the spot to take aggressive actions. But at all events he, as Prime Minister, held the ultimate responsibility; and this imperial confrontation provided further ammunition for the Liberal Party in the election of 1880. In his Midlothian campaign of 1879-80 (see page 42), Gladstone was able to present his hated rival Disraeli as a reckless warmonger, willing to sacrifice morality, lives, and money for mere prestige.

8 Conclusion: Disraeli's Foreign Policy

Disraeli has been both praised and vilified for his foreign policy in general and for his Eastern policy in particular. On the latter, more specific, issue, we have seen that his policies can be interpreted in contrasting ways. There are several reasons for this. In particular, it is impossible to be certain about his opinions and motives.

First, did Disraeli positively desire war with Russia? This is an issue on which the experts have disagreed. Seton-Watson believed that he did indeed wish for war, and that he was lucky that peace was preserved. But the case is certainly not proven. Disraeli was undoubtedly prepared to risk war - and perhaps he should be criticised for this - but he several times insisted that the more willing Britain was to go to the brink of war, the more circumspectly Russia would act. No one can be really sure what was in his mind; but, on the whole, it does seem that he was not a positive warmonger.

Secondly, we need to ask whether Disraeli was correct in his estimation of Russian policy, and in particular whether Russia had aggressive designs both in the Balkans and on India. Disraeli seems to have feared the worst, but, at least according to Seton-Watson, quite wrongly. Certainly there is no evidence that the Tsar intended to invade India. In addition, there is some evidence that the Tsar wished to play a low-key role in the Balkans. Seton-Watson obtained the secret correspondence between Tsar Alexander II, his Chancellor in St Petersburg, and the Russian ambassador in London, Count Shuvalov. In his view, this showed beyond doubt that the Russians were not guilty of the intentions of which Disraeli suspected them and that they had no sinister designs on Constantinople. Yet again the case is not proven. The Tsar may have received pacific advice from St Petersburg and London, but other counsellors spoke with different tongues. For example, his ambassador in Constantinople, Ignatiev, certainly favoured expansion in the Balkans and the capture of the Straits, and he advised the Tsar accordingly. There could be no guarantee that the Tsar would not, in the end, take the advice of the hawks, especially as events served to inflame Panslav feeling. Certainly Ignatiev was able to dominate Russian policy long enough to secure both war with Turkey in 1877 and the harsh treaty of San Stefano in 1878. Perhaps, therefore, Disraeli was right to fear the worst. Another factor, of course, is that the British Prime Minister did not know of the correspondence Seton-Watson unearthed, and therefore many historians consider his criticism of Disraeli to be entirely groundless. In their view the Prime Minister had to act with imperfect knowledge and should be judged only on the facts at his disposal.

For his foreign policy in general, Disraeli has been criticised as an opportunist who had no principles, as for instance in his reaction to the Bulgarian massacre in 1876 or his support of imperialism. He is often described as a selfish politician obsessed with personal and national prestige, even to the point of risking a major war. However, to his supporters, Disraeli was not an opportunist at all: in their view, he was a statesman consistently pursuing not prestige but national greatness and doing so with commendable flexibility and great success.

Commentators on Disraeli's foreign policy have often used terminology which is 'loaded'. What one person may stigmatise as unworthy 'prestige' may be praised by another as commendable 'national greatness'; one person's cynical 'opportunism' becomes another's estimable 'flexibility'; and a run-of-the-mill 'politician' may be elevated into an altogether superior 'statesman'. The language that is used, rather than the facts of the case, are designed to convince people of a particular viewpoint. Yet several obstacles lie in the way of objective judgements.

First, it is very difficult to determine the precise intentions of the Tory leader. If he sought British prestige (or national greatness), should this be judged an unworthy or a legitimate motive? The answer to this question cannot be strictly factual because it is a matter of moral or political judgement. Secondly, in assessing his achievement, how much weight should be given to the short-term as against the long-term consequences of his diplomacy? This is often crucial in determining that important but controversial issue - 'success'. If the former, then the annexation of the Transvaal seemed an immediate success, while a few years later, during the Zulu War, or at the turn of the century during the Boer War, the action was perceived much more problematically. Similarly, if short-term results are examined, the Congress of Berlin may be celebrated as a great personal triumph; but from a longer-term perspective it does not seem nearly so great a settlement. Indeed should the Congress be seen as a success at all? Perhaps, rather than attempting to bolster up the Turks (a policy Salisbury later described as 'backing the wrong horse'), Disraeli should have reversed British policy altogether and sought other means of safeguarding British interests against Russian ambitions in the Balkans. Such reasoning involves the third difficulty in formulating overall judgements on Disraeli's diplomacy - how to estimate the likely results of alternative policies. This is a fascinating issue, but also an extraordinarily difficult one, since no one can ever be fully sure that would have resulted had other courses of actions been pursued. Finally, we also have to ask how far luck, as opposed to good judgement, was a factor in Disraeli's policies. It certainly *was* a factor - after all, the revolution in Turkey in 1876, which rendered the Berlin Memorandum a dead letter, was most fortunate - and therefore it must detract from Disraeli's personal credit in foreign policy, since, by definition, no one is responsible for luck.

It should be clear by this stage that reaching conclusions on Disraeli's foreign policy is an enormously complex undertaking, involving not only the accumulation of knowledge but the formulation of judgements. An examination of the diverse criteria by which judgements are made - as in the previous paragraph - should go a long way towards explaining why historians have often disagreed in their verdicts.

Yet there are also other controversial issues to be considered. First there is the question of whether Disraeli's primary motive in his diplomacy was the wish to influence domestic politics. He himself told Derby in 1871 that it was right that the mind of the political nation 'should be diverted from that morbid spirit of domestic change and criticism, which has ruled us too much for the last forty years'. He was also aware, after the Second Reform Act of 1867, in which he gave the vote to all male householders in the boroughs and so almost doubled the total number of electors, that it was necessary to win votes by appealing in some way to the new mass electorate. Spectacular successes in foreign policy might therefore be one way of staying in office, especially as his years in government after 1874 proved to be a period of trade depression, poor harvests and rising unemployment. One critic in 1878 described his foreign policy as 'Bounce and Bluster ... designed to withdraw public attention from the necessity of domestic reform'. Certainly many members of the public approved of his aggressive policies and the rhetorical flourishes that accompanied them. Perhaps Disraeli's aim therefore, as several historians believe, was to gain for the Conservative Party an enviable reputation as the patriotic party, which put national interests above all other concerns. It may well be that Disraeli's foreign policy was merely an extension of his domestic policy. Certainly he knew the importance of working, whenever possible, with, rather than against, the grain of public opinion; and when he secured successes, he saw the need to milk them for all they were worth. But would he not have reversed his pro-Turkish policy, which was so unpopular around 1876, if his main concern had been domestic political popularity?

Perhaps *Punch* was right: its cartoons regularly depicted Disraeli as the Sphinx, guarding its riddle. Probably he will continue to guard his secrets. We may be certain that his foreign policy will be debated for a long time to come and that highly contrasting verdicts will continue to be made about this enigmatic figure.

Finally, perhaps the most perplexing question of all concerns the conflict between Disraeli and his old rival Gladstone. How much real difference was there between them? All historians are agreed that, in rhetoric and political style, they were poles apart. Yet were there differences of substance? Was Disraeli really the cynical adventurer, compared with Gladstone the high-minded moralist? Was one an imperialist and the other an anti-imperialist? Derby said that Disraeli's policy was one of 'occupy, fortify, grab and bag'; but in reality he had done little to expand British possessions overseas. His imperialism had been more rhetorical than real. Would Gladstone's anti-imperialism, which was certainly embodied in fine rhetoric, be any more real?

Consideration of this issue must await coverage of Gladstone's actions, after he returned to office in 1880, in the next chapter.

Making notes on '*Disraeli and Foreign Policy, 1865-80*'

You will need to compile a full set of notes on the contents of this chapter. Pay most attention to the Eastern Question: this is a complex issue, and so you will need to take detailed notes. Try to distinguish between the actions (about which there is no doubt) and the motives (about which there is plenty). Do not neglect the maps: these will repay careful study and will aid your understanding. The headings and sub-headings should help you to organise your material. Pay particular attention to sections 6(b) and 6(c) on the Congress of Berlin and section 8, the final conclusion: they provide an opportunity for you to reach your own verdicts. It will be a good idea to return to the section on the consequences of the Congress of Berlin after you have read the much fuller accounts of policy after 1878 in the next chapters.

Group discussion should enable you to decide whether you think Disraeli sought 'prestige' or 'national greatness', whether he was opportunistic or merely flexible in his approach, and whether he deserves to be called a statesman. It is also worth debating what is meant by the 'national interest'. Always try to consider who benefited from particular policies.

Another useful way of considering Disraeli is in comparison with Gladstone: hence you will need to consult the next chapter, and in particular its section on the similarities and differences between the two men's foreign policies.

Answering essay questions on '*Disraeli and Foreign Policy, 1865-80*'

Questions on Disraeli's foreign policy tend to be of three main types. They can focus on his foreign policy in general, on the Eastern Question in particular, or on a comparison with Gladstone. For examples of the third issue, see the study guide to Chapter 3.

Consider the following typical questions:

1 Estimate the success of Disraeli's foreign policy between 1874 and 1880.
2 How successful and how statesmanlike was Disraeli's handling of the Eastern Question between 1875 and 1878?
3 To what extent did Disraeli's handling of the Eastern Question further the best interests of Great Britain?
4 How far did Disraeli's external policies promote Britain's power and prestige in the world?

All of these questions are of the same basic character: they are 'quantitative', asking 'how far' or 'to what extent'. This is obvious with 3 and 4; but 1 and 2 are of the same type. 'Estimate the success of Disraeli', for instance, means exactly the same as 'How far was Disraeli successful?' 'How successful', in question 2, means 'to what extent was he successful'. Questions of this type are extremely common, and so it is worth thinking about the best way of tackling them.

Think carefully about question 1. Logically this question, and those like it, can be answered in three different ways: you can say that Disraeli's foreign policy was 100 per cent successful, that it was 100 per cent unsuccessful, or you can opt for some in-between position, arguing that it was partly successful and therefore partly unsuccessful. It is always worth at least considering the 'extreme' positions: after all, a 100 per cent answer will have the virtues of being clear-cut and definite.

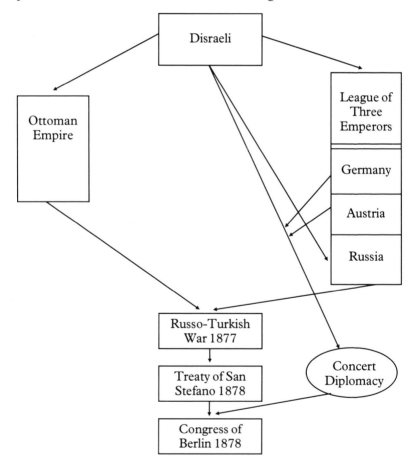

Summary - Disraeli and Foreign Policy, 1865-80

Most often, however, since history is rarely black-and-white, you will probably go for some sort of middle position. To say that it was 'partly successful' will not be definite or ambitious enough. What other, more precise, form of words might be used? Obviously this depends on how successful you think Disraeli was. If there are, in your opinion, only minor and relatively unimportant issues on which he did not succeed, you might perhaps choose the word 'overwhelmingly' to qualify 'successful'. If, on the other hand, you think that successes and failures are even in number and importance, you might choose another term, such as 'balanced' or even 'fifty-fifty'. It does not matter what words you choose so long as their meaning is clear and so long as they fit your interpretation of events: do not be led astray, into an untenable argument, by an ill-judged choice of terminology.

It cannot be emphasised too much that the key to a successful essay is the first paragraph. Never just plunge into an essay and write about the topic: instead you must answer the precise question that has been set, and in the first paragraph you should be reassuring the examiner that you have thought about the question and are answering it directly and relevantly. Hence in the first paragraph of an answer to question 1 you would do three things. First, you would define the terms of the question (especially 'success', an issue taken up on pages 63-66); next, you would break the topic down into smaller sub-divisions, on each of which you would subsequently have a whole paragraph; and, finally, you would outline an argument - and for question 1 this means generalising about the extent to which Disraeli's foreign policy was successful (and, therefore, the degree to which it was not successful). This will probably involve balancing Disraeli's successes against his failures, but do not be afraid to conclude that some aspects of his policies were neither successes nor failures. Alternatively, you might perhaps adopt the judgement that his policies were short-term successes and long-term failures. In fact the arguments/interpretations that could be given are endless. All that is important is that you do have a relevant argument and that you can support it with evidence. At the end of the essay, in the concluding paragraph, return once again to the central issue - the *extent* of success/failure - and hammer home your view. Often you might choose to use forms of words such as 'on the one hand' (followed by a brief rehearsal of the arguments for that view) and 'on the other hand' (followed by evidence for the opposing interpretation), ending with as exact a conclusion as you can formulate.

Examine questions 2-4. What terms would you need to define at the outset of each essay? How could you break down the relevant factual material into coherent sub-divisions? And what form of words would you choose to express your view about the quantitative issues asked in the questions? Your practice on these questions, and those given later in this book, should enable you to tackle unseen questions of this type with real confidence.

Source-based questions on 'Disraeli and Foreign Policy, 1874-80'

1 Disraeli's speech in 1868
Read the extract on page 15 and answer the following questions.
a) Disraeli said that there would be no 'unnecessary' interference in
    Europe. What do you think he meant by this? (2 marks)
b) In what circumstance and for what reasons did Disraeli believe that
    Britain had a 'duty' to interfere in Europe? (3 marks)
c) Illustrate how Disraeli's choice of words showed his pride in his
    nation and its empire. (5 marks)

2 Gladstone on the Bulgarian Horrors
Read the extract on page 20 and answer the following questions.
a) How did Gladstone demonstrate his *moral* repudiation of the Turks
    in this passage? (2 marks)
b) Why do you think that some contemporaries misinterpreted this
    extract and believed that Gladstone wanted to end Turkish rule in
    the whole of the Balkan region? (4 marks)
c) What characteristics of this passage were likely to arouse the
    emotions of its readers? (4 marks)

3 'Neutrality under Difficulties'
Study the cartoon from *Punch* on page 21 and answer the following
questions.
a) Explain the significance of Britannia's gesture. What unspoken
    words does it convey? (3 marks)
b) How adequately does the depiction of Disraeli convey his attitude to
    the Bulgarian massacre? (4 marks)
c) How significant do you find the title of the cartoon? (4 marks)

4 Music Hall Song
Read the lyrics on pages 25-6 and answer the following questions.
a) What would be the probable effects on the audience of the
    description of Russia in the first stanza? Explain your answer.
    (4 marks)
b) What exactly is referred to by the lines 'The Lion did his best to find
    him some excuse/To crawl back to his den again'? (2 marks)
c) How would you describe the mood of the second stanza? In
    particular, do you accept that 'We don't want to fight'? (4 marks)

5 'A Blaze of Triumph'
Study the cartoon from *Punch* on page 29 and answer the following
questions.
a) How apt do you consider this depiction of Disraeli at the Congress of

Berlin as both a tightrope walker and, more generally, a showman? (2 marks)
b) Who is the figure on Disraeli's back? What was the probable intended effect of the cartoonist in depicting him in this way? (3 marks)
c) Explain whether, in your judgement, the cartoon is praising Disraeli or criticising him. (5 marks)

CHAPTER 3

The Foreign Policy of Gladstone, 1880-94

1 The 1880 General Election

The Liberals won a clear majority in 1880. Disraeli thought the tide had turned against his Conservatives largely because of economic factors; but there can be no doubt that Gladstone thundered his attacks primarily against the foreign and imperial policies of his rival. In order to attract maximum publicity, he had decided to contest the marginal seat of Midlothian in Scotland.

In his Midlothian campaigns in 1879 and 1880, to audiences of thousands, Gladstone made outspoken criticisms of all that Disraeli had done in foreign affairs since 1875. He insisted that he had mismanaged Britain's interests, tarnished her honour, and burdened the country by 'mischievous, unauthorised, unprofitable engagements'. He roundly condemned not only his handling of the Eastern Question - the acquisition of Cyprus being 'insane ... an act of duplicity not surpassed and rarely equalled in the history of nations' - but also his involvements outside Europe. Gladstone attacked Disraeli's purchase of shares in the Suez Canal Company as a 'monstrous claim' to control other people's territory just because it was en route to India. As for the wars in Afghanistan and South Africa, they were entirely unjustified. Showing a refreshing lack of national or racial arrogance, the Liberal insisted that 'the sanctity of life in the hill villages of Afghanistan ... is as inviolable in the eye of Almighty God' as that of the inhabitants of Britain; and he condemned the massacre of thousands of Zulus for no offence other than their brave attempt 'to defend against our artillery with their naked bodies their hearths and homes'. In short, Disraeli had conducted a 'sinister foreign policy, deliberately designed to stifle liberty and progress' and to awaken in the British people 'unworthy emotions' such as 'lust for glory, aggressiveness, and chauvinism'. Seldom can political criticisms have been more thorough or unrestrained.

The corollary of this indictment was that a Liberal foreign policy would avoid unnecessary wars and immoral imperial conquests, for which there was no need anyway since the essential strength of England lay 'within the compass of these [British] isles'. Gladstone's own actions would be based squarely on six coherent moral principles:

1 I first give you, gentlemen, what I think [are] the right principles of foreign policy. The first thing is to foster the strength of the Empire by just legislation and economy at home ... and to reserve the strength of the Empire ... for great and worthy occasions abroad.
5 Here is my first principle of foreign policy: good government at

home. My second principle of foreign policy is this - that its aim
ought to be to preserve to the nations of the world ... the blessings
of peace ... My third principle is this ... to strive to cultivate and
maintain, ay, to the very uttermost, what is called the Concert of
10 Europe; to keep the Powers of Europe in union together. And why?
Because by keeping all in union together you neutralize and fetter
and bind up the selfish aims of each. I am not here to flatter
England or any of them. They have selfish aims, as, unfortunately,
15 we in late years have too sadly shown that we too have had selfish
aims; but their common action is fatal to selfish aims. Common
action means common objects; and the only objects for which you
can unite together the Powers of Europe are objects connected
with the common good of them all ... My fourth principle is that
20 you should avoid needless and entangling engagements ... My fifth
principle is this, gentlemen, to acknowledge the equal rights of all
nations ... And the sixth is, that in my opinion ... the foreign policy
of England should always be inspired by the love of freedom.
There should be a sympathy with freedom, a desire to give it scope,
25 founded not upon visionary ideas, but upon the long experience of
many generations within the shores of this happy isle, that in
freedom you lay the firmest foundations of loyalty and order...

Believing that the Almighty had led him to victory, Gladstone
proclaimed that British foreign policy should be based upon the precept
'do as we would be done by'. Only a moral foreign policy fostering
brotherhood - rather than Disraeli's search for selfish national
aggrandisement - would, he believed, produce the ultimate goals of
humankind, justice and peace on earth. The question, of course, was
whether Gladstone, now once more Liberal leader and Prime Minister,
would be able to live up to such lofty ideals. His periods in office from
1880 to 1885, and again in 1886 and 1892-5, put his principles to a
severe test.

2 The Impact of Gladstone: Change and Continuity

In 1880 Gladstone was not concerned, as Disraeli had been in 1874, to
seize the initiative in foreign affairs. Nevertheless, many expected, after
Midlothian, that he would revolutionise British foreign policy. Surely he
would pursue a policy of peace and justice in external affairs. After all, he
was at heart an anti-imperialist: he had no real enthusiasm for the British
Empire, believing that people had a right to govern themselves. He also
disliked the pomp and ceremony of empire, which he believed to be
vainglorious. Furthermore, he regarded the search for national prestige
as a childish, unworthy pursuit: he saw no contradiction between
Britain's interests and those of the rest of the world. Not surprisingly,
therefore, there were indeed to be significant changes in Britain's foreign

and imperial policies.

However, there were signs that Gladstone's external policy would show not only change but also a measure of continuity with that of his predecessor. For instance, while Gladstone would have liked to cede Cyprus ('a valueless encumbrance') to Greece, he was persuaded by his Foreign Secretary, Lord Granville, that public opinion would not favour such a move. The Turkish Sultan, Abdul Hamid, who had every reason to resent Gladstone, might also be expected to complain by every means possible at the transfer of territory to which he had a legal claim. There seemed to be a great difference between refusing to extend the Empire and actually giving up colonies, a distinction Gladstone endorsed when he explained in 1881 that Liberals like himself, while 'opposed to imperialism', were 'devoted to the empire'. It does not seem, for instance, that he even considered giving up India, although, characteristically, he did insist that the sub-continent should 'be governed for her own benefit not for England's'.

Yet few, around 1880, would have guessed that, though Gladstone was soon to turn the other cheek to potential enemies on several occasions, he was also to use the threat of war and actual warfare as instruments of policy. Furthermore, the British Empire was actually to expand far more under Gladstone than it had under Disraeli. As a result, many have judged that Gladstone's 'principles', expounded upon in his verbose and tireless style, were simply so much hot air and that he was guilty of rank hypocrisy. How may we explain this continuity of policy?

There are several explanations. First, it should be noted that foreign policy was not decided solely by Gladstone. He had, of necessity, to consult his colleagues. A prime minister, under the British constitution, is not a dictator: he has to proceed with the agreement of his cabinet. It should also be remembered that Gladstone was exceedingly busy with other areas of policy - especially Ireland, an issue with which some came to believe him positively obsessed - and so could not devote himself solely to external affairs. Indeed, until the end of 1882, he was not only Prime Minister but also Chancellor of the Exchequer. It is also true that his health was poor, especially in 1883 and 1884, so that he could not take an active part in all cabinet discussions. Furthermore, he had to battle against the wishes of the Queen, who regarded him and all his works with a disgust that bordered on the pathological. (Small wonder that Gladstone once said that Victoria 'is enough to kill any man'!) Two further factors are also important. One is, quite simply, the course of events. Indeed some historians believe that events controlled him far more than he controlled them. The Almighty may have brought Gladstone to power, but if so He made it extremely difficult for him to solve foreign policy problems in a Christian manner. The other is the failure of his attempts to revive the Concert of Europe.

a) The Concert of Europe

Gladstone believed sincerely in co-operation with Europe. He regarded Europeans not as inferior foreigners, who did not have the supreme good fortune to be English, but as equals. He himself spoke several European languages, including French, German, Italian and Greek (in contrast to Disraeli, who knew only English); he visited the continent many times and had genuine friends there; and he had a profound reverence for European civilisation. In 1880 and 1881 Gladstone worked hard to set up a new Concert of Europe, and there were some promising signs that it might work well. In particular, he managed to form a sound working relationship with France, and he hoped that their two governments - both liberal parliamentary regimes - would co-operate for the good of the whole of Europe. He even acquiesced, though with some misgivings, when the French seized Tunis in 1881. This 'liberal alliance' might then be extended to include other Powers, so that the Congress ideal would be achieved. A union of all would, as he said at Midlothian, 'bind up the selfish aims of each'. Yet there was one major problem: his conception of international relations ran completely counter to that of the German Chancellor, Bismarck.

Neither Britain nor Germany had territorial ambitions in Europe, both being satisfied Powers broadly concerned to maintain the status quo, and so it might have seemed that there was a possibility of fruitful cooperation between them, as at the Congress of Berlin in 1878. But Gladstone and Bismarck were vividly contrasting characters who were deeply suspicious of each other. The British Prime Minister was not quite sure what to make of the German Chancellor, though he disapproved of his abandonment of free trade and of his policy of giving German liberals only the semblance, and not the reality, of political power. Bismarck, on the other hand, knew exactly what he thought of his British opposite number - he was a moralising prig, fit only for making up speeches and chopping down trees, inferior to Disraeli by far. Not surprisingly, perhaps, the two men also espoused different means to ensure stability within Europe. Gladstone favoured the Concert system; but Bismarck believed that international conferences would, by their very nature, fail to achieve decisive action. They would produce speeches, resolutions and weak compromises. He much preferred to secure his aims in Europe by secret diplomacy which he himself could dominate.

Gladstone had little hope of reviving the Concert because Bismarck successfully formed a series of alliances designed to foster German foreign policy aims. Bismarck wanted both to isolate the French, so that they could not fight a war of revenge after their defeat by the Prussians in 1871, and to prevent Russia and Austria coming to blows due to divergent interests in the Balkans. To achieve these ends, he signed a series of alliances.

Bismarck's Alliances

1879   the Dual (Austro-German) Alliance, a long-lasting alliance.

1881   the League of Three Emperors (Germany, Austria and Russia), also known as the *Dreikaiserbund*. This agreement was for three years. It was renewed in 1884, but not in 1887.

1882   the Triple Alliance (Germany, Austria and Italy), adding Italy to the Dual Alliance.

1887   the Reinsurance Treaty (Germany and Russia), a three-year agreement, replacing the *Dreikaiserbund*, which had ended because of Austro-Russian disagreements over the Balkans.

These alliances made sure that there was a balance of power (or perhaps 'balance of tension') in Europe which did, for a time, keep the peace; but, almost automatically, they thwarted Gladstone's hopes for a more 'open' style of diplomacy. Bismarck's profoundly pessimistic notion, that states would only stay at peace if they feared one another enough, prevailed over Gladstone's essentially optimistic view that co-operation could be wholehearted and unforced. Hence when crises emerged for Britain - especially in Egypt, but also with Russia over Afghanistan - Gladstone had to use traditional weapons, including force, instead of being able to rely on Concert diplomacy. Indeed Bismarck seemed to delight in obstructing Gladstone's efforts to revive the Concert. He also believed that if he could obstruct the solution of British problems outside Europe the British Prime Minister would be less able to meddle in European affairs. As Bismarck's son once wrote, the German Chancellor's aim was 'to squash Gladstone against the wall, so that he can yap no more.'

3 Turkey

Gladstone began his second ministry with a reputation for being profoundly anti-Turkish, especially because of his reaction to the Bulgarian massacre of 1876 (see page 20). Indeed he soon decided to take firm action against the Turks, who had, so far, refused to honour undertakings made at the Congress of Berlin to cede land to Montenegro and Greece. Gladstone organised a naval demonstration off the coast of Albania in September 1880, and - typically - he did so not unilaterally but with the support of the European Powers, authorised by a special conference of ambassadors which met in Berlin in 1880. The action upset the Queen and failed to have the desired effect on the Sultan, but at least Gladstone was attempting to force Turkey to obey international law and, at the same time, to make a reality of the Concert of Europe. He then proposed firmer joint action against Turkey, an expedition to seize the port of Smyrna and coerce the Sultan into compliance. France and Italy approved, but Bismarck jeered that he would merely 'pray' for the Smyrna expedition. The Austrian government was fearful that Gladstone wanted eventually to destroy Turkish rule in the Balkans, a development which conflicted with Austria's desire to maintain the status quo, and so Vienna also refused support. Austria had co-operated with Disraeli against Russia at the Congress of Berlin, but there could be no similar alignment with Gladstone. Austria was careful not to endanger its close links with Germany, which it viewed as its guarantee of international security. Turkey too began to look to Germany - not, as hitherto, to Britain - for support, and a German military mission arrived in Constantinople in 1882.

Multilateral action against the Sultan was thus vetoed. However, on this occasion the Turkish government gave in, before disunity among the Powers was apparent, and arranged for the transfer of land. There can be no doubt that, in this sphere, Gladstone was working hard to make a reality of the Concert and to live up to his Midlothian promises, but the omens for the future of European co-operation were not good. Instead it was Bismarck's conception of the future which was coming to pass.

4 Afghanistan

In opposition, Gladstone had disapproved of British policy in Afghanistan, describing the conflict of 1879, caused by the policy of the Viceroy Lord Lytton (see page 32), as 'a war as frivolous as ever was waged in the history of man'. Now a new viceroy was appointed, and one of a very different character. He was Lord Ripon (1880-4), who condemned Lytton as heartily as Gladstone had done. But it was far from easy for the new men to extricate themselves from Afghanistan. Before they had decided how to act, British forces were attacked at several points. It would have been fatally easy to meet force with force, but Gladstone decided to negotiate instead, and soon a new deal was struck with the Amir. Britain was given control of several strategically important points connecting Afghanistan with India, including the Khyber Pass, while recognising the independence of the country. Russia seemed content that Afghanistan should be a buffer state between themselves and the British in India, neither side having control. Hence things were working out well for Gladstone, and there seemed no contradiction between his principles and Britain's national interests. Perhaps policy had not been revolutionised, but it had certainly been substantially modified.

Yet a few years later Anglo-Russian relations deteriorated. The Russians, who failed to co-operate with Britain in delineating the Afghan border, began building railways close to Afghan territory, and in March

1885 a border clash occurred at Penjdeh. The Liberal cabinet decided on action: it secured a massive grant of £11 million from parliament and prepared to despatch 25,000 troops from India. The government even had posters printed, announcing that a war with Russia had begun. Britain certainly seemed closer to a major war than at any time since 1878. Yet there were no allies in sight. Indeed Germany, rallying support from France and Italy, issued a warning to the Turkish Sultan not to open the Straits to Britain (from which the British fleet might have entered the Black Sea to attack vulnerable Russian ports). At last the Concert of Europe seemed to exist, but - ironically - it was working against Gladstone. Nevertheless, the Russians had no real wish for war and in May a preliminary arbitration agreement was drawn up which was finalised later by the Conservatives, a domestic crisis having unseated the Liberals in June 1885. Another pause then occurred in the so-called 'Great Game', the struggle for supremacy between the British and Russians in this part of the world. Gladstone's policy had thus been successful, but there were signs, with his threat of force, that his principles had been sacrificed. Certainly Gladstone, like Disraeli before him, had been prepared to run the risk of war with Russia. Yet he himself stated that this was not immoral: he was no pacifist (believing war always to be wrong) and, on this occasion, he believed that a firm policy was fully justified. He argued that, in defence of the Afghans, 'We must do our best to have right done in this matter'.

5 South Africa

In this area too there were early successes. In 1880 Gladstone sacked Sir Bartle Frere, whose policy towards the Zulus he so disliked. Yet he did not, as the Boers hoped and as he had implied at Midlothian, reverse the annexation of the Transvaal which the previous Conservative administration had brought about (see page 33). Hence the Boers, now freed from the Zulu menace, decided to take matters into their own hands. In December 1880, in defiance of Britain, they declared a republic. How would Gladstone's government react to what was in effect a rebellion? Should there be coercion or concession?

a) Gladstone's Cabinet

The cabinet was divided on this issue, as on so many others. There were several ministers who habitually opposed positive actions: one was the Foreign Secretary, Lord Granville, who generally tried to dissuade his Prime Minister from taking the initiative, and another was the Colonial Secretary, Lord Derby (the Conservative Foreign Secretary who, before his resignation in 1878, had done his best to deter Disraeli from aggression). This group wanted to accept what had happened by formally reversing the annexation and agreeing that the Transvaal should be independent. But there were others in the cabinet, and the country, who favoured firmness. The most important of these was Lord Hartington, who had been leader of the Liberal Party during Gladstone's semi-retirement from 1874 to 1880. As the foremost Whig in the government and a disciple of Palmerston, he believed that resolute action was necessary to teach the Boers a lesson and discourage rebels elsewhere in the Empire. Another group agreed with this prescription but from a different motive: they argued that the rebels should be brought to heel in order that Britain might safeguard the rights of the black Africans in the Transvaal. Fierce debates took place, but in the end Gladstone decided to acquiesce in the Boers' action and to recognise the republic.

b) The Conventions

However, early in 1881, before Gladstone's decision could be announced, the Boers annihilated a small British force at Majuba Hill. Britain's High Commissioner at the Cape complained of 'good lives ... thrown away by idiotic leadership'. The first Boer War had begun. Sections of British public opinion loudly demanded retaliatory action,

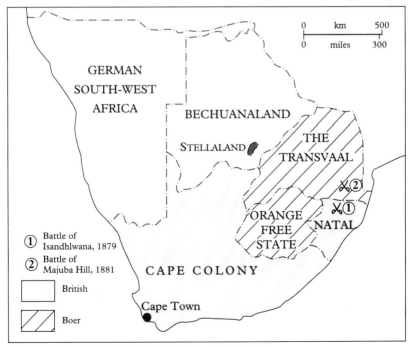

A map of South Africa, circa 1884

and so did the hawks in the cabinet. Yet Gladstone asserted himself and insisted that Britain should put aside 'unworthy emotions' and not seek vengeance. He was prepared to defy the Queen in particular and public opinion in general in the interests of morality and to follow a magnanimous - and, it must also be said, an eminently cheap - policy. As a result, the war was over almost as soon as it had started, and in April 1881, in the Convention of Pretoria, the British government allowed the Transvaal to become an independent republic, subject to what was called the 'suzerainty' of the British Crown. No one knew what this term meant, and differing interpretations were to cause trouble in the future, but there can be no doubt that Gladstone had stoutly adhered to his Midlothian ideals. The circumstances of his imperial retreat, however, allowed critics to say that he had not acted on principle at all but had merely bowed to force. Yet at least a period of calm returned to South Africa.

But further troubles followed in 1884. The settlers in the Transvaal moved westwards into Stellaland, making war on the local chiefs, and it seemed likely that they would advance into Bechuanaland, hitherto unoccupied by Europeans. This would conflict with the aims of the British settlers in Cape Colony by cutting off their northward expansion (see the map on page 49). Many Britons, including leading figures at the Cape such as Cecil Rhodes, were convinced that the leader of the Transvaal, Paul Kruger, wished to strangle Cape Colony and achieve a South Africa in which the Boers were dominant. Amid signs that the two ambitious groups of settlers, already bitter rivals, might come to blows, Gladstone's government was urged to take some definite action, especially since the Cape was still of strategic importance as a staging post on the route to India - see the cartoon from *Punch* on page 51. Typically, Gladstone called a conference in London, where the 1881 Convention was replaced by a new agreement; but it was not a conference between equals. In fact, in the London Convention, the British government insisted not only upon establishing a veto over the Transvaal's foreign policy but upon annexing Bechuanaland. They had no positive wish to acquire new land, Liberal ministers insisted, and indeed Lord Derby described Bechuanaland as 'of no value to us'; but they claimed that the annexation was necessary in the interests of stability and peace. A further motive arose due to the fact that Germany had recently acquired South-West Africa, and it was deemed wise to take Bechuanaland in order to separate this new Power in Africa from the discontented but ambitious Boers in the Transvaal.

These arrangements solved the immediate problem. But they made the Boers more resentful than before. The settlement therefore looked unlikely to last long - especially since, in 1885, Boers infiltrated Bechuanaland anyway. An energetic younger minister, Joseph Chamberlain, urged that the Transvaal must be made to respect the Convention, by force if necessary; but Gladstone refused to take action.

A TERRIBLE THREAT!

Mr. W. E. G. "LOOK HERE, MY CHRISTIAN FRIEND. YOU'VE THREATENED TO HORSEWHIP OUR FORCES; YOU'VE VIOLATED OUR TREATY; YOU'VE MARCHED INTO STELLALAND; AND YOU'VE PULLED DOWN OUR FLAG. A LITTLE MORE,—AND—AND—*YOU'LL ROUSE THE BRITISH LION!!*"

A terrible Threat, Punch, *11 October 1884*

Beset by other problems, he simply allowed the issue to simmer. It later began to boil, when the discovery of gold began to transform the Transvaal into the dominant economic power in South Africa - but it was future governments which had to wrestle with these matters.

It seems that the policy of Gladstone's government was designed to prevent trouble in South Africa, and that the acquisition of Bechuanaland was merely a by-product of this laudable aim. But ideals of non-intervention and self-determination had been overruled. Some historians have even speculated that the policy which Gladstone followed might indeed have been pursued by virtually any British administration, in that ideals were not paramount. It is true that the Liberals did have a moral justification for their actions, humanitarians - and some local chiefs - having urged them to annex Bechuanaland to prevent the tribes there falling under the domination of the Boers. Yet these promptings alone did not motivate British actions. Clearly, in the complex real world, it was proving difficult to translate principle into policy.

6 Egypt

Nothing did so much to convince his critics (and many historians) that Gladstone was a humbug as his relations with Egypt. In 1882 the Liberal apostle of peace - who stood for non-intervention and self-determination and who believed that the path to empire was the road to ruin - invaded Egypt and, in effect, added it to the British Empire. How was it that he acted so markedly against his principles?

The root cause of the problems in Egypt was financial instability. Disraeli had saved the Khedive's regime from bankruptcy with his purchase of shares in 1875. But Britain's £4 million proved only a stop-gap and, before Gladstone became premier in 1880, not only had the Khedive been forced to abdicate in favour of his more pliant son but an Anglo-French commission had been set up to supervise the country's finances and make Egypt solvent again. That shrewd observer Lord Salisbury decided that this dual control in Egypt was better than either a British monopoly, which might force the French into a war with Britain, or renunciation, which might allow the French to control - and possibly block - the route to India.

In 1880 the country's finances were still in a chronically poor state. After revenue had been laid aside to pay interest on debts, there was simply not enough money to pay for both internal administration and the army. The financial commissioners therefore forced the new Khedive (Tewfik) to sack thousands of army officers to stave off bankruptcy. But this led to troubles with the army, whose leaders organised a nationalist campaign against domination by the foreigners and their puppet ruler. In September 1881 the colonels under Arabi Pasha surrounded the royal palace and forced the Khedive to dismiss his government and restore the army to its former strength. Here was a real challenge to Anglo-French influence in Egypt, especially as the officers enjoyed considerable popular support. The French were aggrieved: they had the largest financial stake in Egypt, and they took pride in the Suez Canal, which they had built. The British were also worried. Gladstone feared that the country might soon descend into anarchy, and if this proved to be the case then the security of the Suez Canal - so vital for British shipping - would be in doubt.

The Prime Minister's first reaction was characteristically low-key. He even judged that these signs of nationalist awakening might bode well for the future: 'Egypt for the Egyptians' might provide the ultimate solution to the Egyptian question. Certainly he had no thoughts of an invasion to reassert control, and he wrote to Foreign Secretary Granville that he wished to act with 'a *minimum* of interference'. True to his Midlothian principles, Gladstone believed that the issue must involve the Concert of Europe, not individual Powers acting for themselves, and a conference was called at Constantinople. Most European nations had financial stakes in Egypt, but Bismarck had no intention of seeing the revival of the Concert system and so the conference failed. Nevertheless, Gladstone insisted that if some sort of expedition had to be sent eventually it should be a Turkish one, Egypt being a province of the Ottoman Empire; failing that, it should be Anglo-French; but in no circumstances should it be a solely British affair. When the French decided to send a strong note of warning to the nationalists that they had to accept European financial control or face the consequences, Gladstone was opposed at first. He accepted ultimately only because he felt it necessary to defer to majority opinion in his cabinet, and only after Granville insisted that the note 'was to strengthen the Government of Egypt and maintain the existing order of things'. Yet when it was sent, in January 1882, the nationalists reacted far more aggressively than anticipated, and an extreme nationalist government was installed with Arabi as Minister of War. But, even so, Gladstone opposed invasion. Instead, the British and the French arranged to stage a naval demonstration off the port of Alexandria, believing that the nationalists would be overawed by the mere sight of European ships. Yet in point of fact these naive hopes badly misfired: anti-European feelings were only increased, so much so that in two days, in June 1882, about 50 Europeans were killed and the British Consul was badly wounded. Events seemed to have reached crisis point.

Still Gladstone and Granville were against an invasion. They tried to get the Turkish Sultan to intervene and also arranged for a meeting of the European Powers to consider the matter. But their own cabinet was divided. In particular Lord Hartington came out strongly in favour of action, and several other ministers had also been persuaded in favour of firmness by the riots in Alexandria. They saw Arabi as a military adventurer, not a national leader trying to free his country. Indeed

Hartington threatened to resign unless an invasion of some sort was authorised. Gladstone was at an impasse. But he could not procrastinate much longer, as either the French might act on their own and assume control of a territory vital to British interests or, alternatively, the nationalists might endanger the canal zone. For a time, as one minister noted in his diary, Gladstone, Granville and the veteran radical John Bright 'stood alone against the rest of the Cabinet in supporting a let-alone policy'. Then Granville gave way, and finally Gladstone bowed before majority opinion on a crucial issue. The British admiral, judging that his fleet off Alexandria was in danger from coastal defences which were being extended, asked permission to bombard the batteries if work on them was not stopped. Now he was given the decisive green light by the politicians: he could send an ultimatum to the local people.

The cabinet hoped that the ultimatum would solve the problem not exacerbate it. But in fact the admiral exceeded his orders. He had been authorised to demand that work be stopped on the local forts, but instead he insisted they be removed altogether. On 11 July 1882 he bombarded the coastal defences when the ultimatum expired, sparking off widespread anti-British riots and a declaration of war on Britain by Arabi. The canal zone was now in real danger, and everyone - apart from

Gladstone Invading Egypt, The Gladstone A.B.C.

Bright, who resigned - was convinced that Britain had to act. All that was in doubt was the form action should take. Gladstone wanted a joint naval police action with the French - and possibly the Italians - to safeguard the canal zone, while the hawks in his cabinet wanted a larger expedition to destroy Arabi. Soon it was the latter who won out in cabinet, and it was decided to send British forces to Cyprus and Malta to be in readiness. Parliament then voted by a huge majority (275 to 19) to raise £2.3 million to pay for the expedition. The Tories might have been expected to vote for a 'forward' policy, but many Liberals were only convinced of the need to send an expedition by a fine speech from Gladstone. He told the Commons that the canal was vulnerable and that it could never be protected so long as Egypt remained in anarchy, and that therefore Britain had to act, in concert with other powers if possible but alone if necessary. He also worked up MPs' emotions by stressing the atrocities that had been committed against Europeans. It was a masterly performance, all the more convincing because of Gladstone's reputation as a great humanitarian who would not intervene lightly in the affairs of another state. Invasion could therefore be interpreted as not so much a disreputable military adventure as a moral punishment for wrongdoing (see the cartoon on page 54).

In August 1882 British forces landed in Egypt. It had been impossible to arrange joint action with the Concert of Europe and, at the last minute, the French government withdrew support when the Chamber of Deputies voted against the venture. Because relations with Germany continued to be menacing, the French judged that Egypt was not a vital enough interest to warrant their involvement. Britain's action was thus unilateral. It was also highly successful. In September the army won an important victory at Tel el Kebir and then occupied Cairo.

Gladstone insisted that he had not actually 'occupied' Egypt. He had merely 'intervened', and he called for 'withdrawal ... as early as possible' since anything else 'would be absolutely at variance with all the principles and views of Her Majesty's Government'. But Britain could not withdraw immediately: first the ringleaders of the revolt had to be put on trial and the Khedive installed again on the throne (though now with a British Consul-General to 'advise' him). And even that was not enough: Britain had to make sure that the Khedivate was stable and that the Canal zone was secure, aims which necessitated the training of a new Egyptian police force and army. In addition, a new form of financial control had to be established, to make sure that the European bondholders received their debt repayments in full and on time, and so a new loan had to be negotiated with Britain as guarantor. In 1883 Gladstone said that he would leave within a year providing the Great Powers would accept British influence in Egypt, not attempting to dominate the area themselves, and would guarantee free passage along the canal. His ideal was that Egypt would become a sort of 'Eastern Belgium', whose neutrality was respected by all. But France refused and so did Germany. Hence, in effect, British imperial rule had come to Cairo, and under a prime minister, Gladstone, who was a self-styled anti-imperialist. What Robinson and Gallagher have termed Gladstone's 'Egyptian bondage' had begun.

a) Egyptian Invasion: Summary of Causes

John Bright had resigned over British actions in Egypt, insisting that

> the moral law is intended not only for individual life, but for the life and practice of States in their dealings with one another. I think that in the present case there has been a manifest violation of International Law and of the moral law.

The doctrine of responsibility which Gladstone had formerly preached was thus preached back at him. So how was it that he ended up taking actions which seemed so contrary to his intentions? Certainly he had not been suddenly converted to new principles: he still believed in the 'moral law'. It should also be noted that he had tried hard to avoid intervention if it were possible or, if it were not, to act in concert with other Powers. Indeed he always insisted that though Britain had acted alone she was acting on behalf of the Concert. He undoubtedly had bad luck in being presented with a situation which proved so intractable and in having, as cabinet colleagues, men of different principles from himself. As Robinson and Gallagher wrote, in their masterly study *Africa and the Victorians,* it was events in Africa not a new spirit in Britain which produced intervention. The leading figures in the government had not intended what happened: 'They muddled and drifted with events'. The occupation thus owed more to circumstances than to intention, so that Gladstone was a very reluctant imperialist. But, in the end, the politician prevailed over the moralist: beset by endless difficulties, Gladstone had decided to keep his government together and stay in office rather than resign.

b) The Sudan

The invasion of Egypt constituted one charge against Gladstone by those who had been impressed by his Midlothian speeches; a second charge was the occupation of the country. Soon a third was levelled because he became involved with the Sudan, which the Egyptians claimed was theirs. Yet to others, including probably most members of the public, action in Egypt was popular, and many people could not understand why the prime minister was so reluctant to send forces into the Sudan. Clearly Gladstone could not please all the people all the time, and soon he was wondering whether he could please any of the people any of the time.

Britain's Consul-General in Cairo, Sir Evelyn Baring (nicknamed 'Over-Baring' by his subordinates), believed that the British presence would be needed for some time in Egypt, otherwise anarchy would return and the French might step in. He also advised that Britain should help the Egyptians make good their claim to the neighbouring territory of the Sudan. Foreign domination in Egypt was undermining Egyptian authority in the Sudan, which was already coming under attack because of a revolt by Mohammed Ahmed, the son of a Dongolese boat builder, otherwise known as the 'Mahdi', an extreme Muslim religious leader whose arrival was said to have been foretold by Islamic lore. Baring insisted that if the Egyptians tamely pulled out of their Sudanese base at Khartoum, the Khedive would become so unpopular that his regime might totter and conceivably fall. Indeed the Mahdi, whose forces were taking all before them and who had annihilated an Egyptian army of 10,000 men at the end of 1883, might even attack Egypt. The result of such calamities, he warned, could well be that Britain would have to support Egypt for longer than anyone envisaged, perhaps for ten years or more. Today this would be described as a 'no win situation' for Gladstone, but Baring strongly advised the government to adopt the lesser evil by conquering the Sudan. What would Gladstone do? Queen Victoria urged him to wage war against the 'wild Arabs' and warned him that he would not be forgiven if he did not rescue the Sudan as soon as possible from 'murder, and rapine, and utter confusion'. Here was another challenge to his Midlothian principles.

Gladstone's sympathies were very much against intervening in the Sudan, whose inhabitants he once described, in typically moralistic fashion, as 'a people rightly struggling to be free'. He also reckoned that the conquest of the Sudan would impose intolerable financial burdens on the Khedive. There was division, as always, in his cabinet. However, in January 1884 Baring's advice was rejected. Gladstone insisted that Britain would guarantee only Egypt's own borders and that there should be a policy of non-interference in the Sudan. Orders were therefore given for the last Egyptian forces to withdraw. Yet Gladstone did agree to send General Charles Gordon - a man of vast experience in China and the Sudan - to supervise the evacuation of the Egyptian garrisons still in Khartoum. This was in fact a fatal mistake, for Gordon was a fervent imperialist and religious fanatic. Baring considered him 'half cracked', and certainly he was not the man to undertake a policy of which he disapproved. Disobeying orders, and underestimating the enemy, he delayed in the Sudan until he could encounter the Mahdi. By March 1884 he and the small force at his disposal were surrounded by the Mahdi's troops in Khartoum. The siege lasted ten months, and once again the British government came under pressure to intervene. Would Gladstone agree to despatch a rescue mission?

Queen Victoria was adamant that Gordon, for whom she 'trembled', must be saved, but the government made no pronouncement on the issue. Debate on whether to send a relief expedition rumbled on throughout the spring and early summer of 1884, by which time virtually every member of the Liberal government was heartily sick and tired of involvement in north Africa. There were already enough crises to face, over Ireland and over electoral reform, without these troubles. Gladstone himself was against action. Well aware that Gordon had disobeyed orders and so had no one but himself to blame, the Prime Minister saw no reason to risk British lives and spend taxpayers' money by entering Sudanese territory. Yet several members of the cabinet decided to resign if no action was taken, and so in August parliament was asked to vote £300,000 to pay for a rescue expedition. When it finally arrived in Khartoum, in February 1885, General Gordon's headless corpse was found. He had only been dead for a few days.

Gladstone and his government bore the brunt of a tremendous outpouring of criticism, for Gordon had been inflated in the popular imagination into the archetypal Victorian hero. Several full-length plays were staged to celebrate his heroism, and he was the subject of a spate of adulatory biographies. As for Gladstone, many members of the public decided that the G.O.M. (Grand Old Man) of British politics was really the M.O.G. (Murderer of Gordon). According to a popular song of the time, a place was being reserved for Gladstone in Hell between Pontius Pilate and Judas Iscariot. It even looked for a time as though the government might fall. But Gladstone tacked before the wind. When the public demanded revenge against the Mahdi, his cabinet agreed to send a punitive force. He also, in reply to a vote of censure from the Conservatives, came close to admitting that mistakes had been made in both Egypt and the Sudan.

1 I have often owned in this House that the difficulties of the case have passed entirely beyond the limits of such political and military difficulties as I have known in the course of an experience of half a century. Therefore, I do not ask the House to believe that what we
5 have done is necessarily right, but as to honesty of purpose, painful as the course we have had to pursue has been to me, I felt that we had no alternative. We have been bound from the time that we first covenanted to keep the Khedive upon his Throne, and at no point have we had before us the choice or the possibility of return ...
10 There has been no want of honesty, but possibly want of judgment has made me at last a party of these decisions, which, sad and deplorable as they may have been in themselves, were yet unavoidable under the circumstances and at the moment when we were called upon to take them.

The steam was taken out of the situation, and the uproar over Gordon's death soon subsided. Gladstone stoutly resisted calls from the Whigs in his party to secure the whole of the Sudan for the British Empire, and even the expedition against the Mahdi's Dervishes was cancelled when the Penjdeh incident conjured up the spectre of a war with Russia (see page 48). Events in Afghanistan - or perhaps, Gladstone believed, the hand of the Almighty - thus provided the perfect excuse to withdraw from a commitment which the Prime Minister wanted to slough off anyway. In April 1885 the government ordered that the Sudan be evacuated.

7 Imperial Expansion

Many critics believed that Gladstone was implacably hostile to the British Empire. They also thought that his attempts to give Home Rule to Ireland might prove to be the beginning of the end of the Empire, but in this they were quite wrong. His Home Rule Bills (of 1886 and 1893) failed to get through parliament, and the Empire expanded rather than contracted while he was Prime Minister. The invasion of Egypt, and involvements in the Sudan, extended the area of British dominance in the world - what is sometimes called 'informal' rather than 'formal' empire - and in 1885 Bechuanaland became a British protectorate. There were other imperial acquisitions as well. Part of Somaliland was annexed, part of New Guinea and, in 1894, the whole of Uganda. This was the period of the beginning of the 'Scramble for Africa', when European Powers partitioned the so-called 'dark continent' not only because they positively wanted new territory but to prevent rival Powers acquiring land. Gladstone had no wish for new colonies and, unlike many other politicians, did not regard them as highly prestigious status symbols, but his government did not stand aside. Britain's existing imperial possessions meant, almost automatically, that she came into contact - and usually conflict - with expansionist Powers like Bismarck's Germany. It was therefore necessary for Britain to attend a conference at the end of 1884 in Berlin, where ground rules were devised for the occupation of West Africa. The conference helped ensure that this portion of the continent was partitioned speedily and peacefully. The Concert of Europe was thus functioning effectively, but to produce a result entirely counter to Gladstone's Midlothian principles.

The Premier undoubtedly disliked the new climate of aggressive imperial expansion. Indeed, as essentially a mid-Victorian, he seemed increasingly out of touch as the 1880s wore on. For instance, the historian Sir John Seeley captured the popular imagination when, in his *Expansion of England* of 1883, he argued that the 'clue' which explained the pattern of British history over the previous two centuries was not the development of liberty but the growth of the Empire. It seemed, therefore, that Britain's destiny lay in an ever-larger empire. But to Gladstone such ideas were merely bizarre. Many began to think that he had outlived his usefulness.

8 Foreign Policy in 1886 and 1892-4

Gladstone was Prime Minister on two further occasions, but foreign policy did not feature significantly in either of them. Indeed he seemed to favour British isolation more than in his earlier administrations. His main priority was Irish Home Rule. In 1886 he told his Foreign Secretary, Lord Rosebery, that it was 'very desirable, while we have this big Irish business on hand, that no other important issue of disturbing character should be raised'. Ireland did indeed loom large hereafter in Gladstone's premierships, especially since it was an issue which was destined to split the Liberal party. In 1886 a group of 'Liberal Unionists' separated themselves from the official Party and, later, joined with the Conservatives. These included figures like Joseph Chamberlain, who called not only for the maintenance of the union between Britain and Ireland but also for imperial expansion. Gladstone, who continued to oppose the acquisition of territory for its own sake, had rid himself of troublesome colleagues. Yet there was still a 'Liberal imperialist' wing in his party, led by Rosebery, whose adherents found it difficult to work with the ageing Premier. In 1894 there was a sharp tussle between Gladstone and Rosebery over whether or not Britain should annex Uganda, the Prime Minister in the end bowing to the wishes of the younger man. Unlike this imperialist faction, Gladstone, who became more radical the older he got, favoured disarmament rather than rearmament, and by 1894 he found himself becoming more and more isolated within his own party. 'The world of today,' he lamented, 'is not the world in which I was bred and trained and have principally lived'. He resigned at the age of 85 - and permanently this time - over calls for larger naval spending. Characteristically, the Queen did not consult him about a replacement, and she chose Lord Rosebery.

9 Conclusion

Several fundamental questions arise from a study of Gladstone's foreign policy. First, historians have often asked how far his policies differed from those of his rival.

a) Gladstone and Disraeli Compared

Until recently, Disraeli and Gladstone were generally portrayed as total opposites in Victorian politics, including foreign policy. For instance, Disraeli was depicted as standing for British greatness and prestige, Gladstone for lofty ideals. The former was said to have a Machiavellian cunning which allowed him to ignore morality, while it was argued that the latter sincerely believed Christian principles should govern conduct between states, as well as between individuals. Alongside these deep-seated differences went a corresponding contrast in rhetoric and style. Disraeli was inclined to swagger and boast; Gladstone was likely to beat his breast and thunder sermons from the despatch box. 'Rarely in our history,' R.W. Seton-Watson wrote, 'has there been so complete a contrast between two notable protagonists'. Small wonder, then, that the two men heartily disliked each other or that, according to this interpretation, their foreign policies were substantially different. Disraeli favoured propping up Turkey in the Near East, while Gladstone wished Turkey to quit the Balkans and favoured the emergence of independent Slav nations. Disraeli therefore acted unilaterally as an English nationalist, while Gladstone sought to achieve co-operation through the Concert of Europe. Similarly, Disraeli wanted to expand the Empire, while Gladstone favoured self-determination and saw no value in more colonies.

However, almost all recent accounts have tended to stress not the differences but the similarities between the two men. Historians who adopt this approach tend to play down differences in style and rhetoric, arguing that the verbal pyrotechnics between Gladstone and Disraeli, to which historians once attached so much importance, have distracted attention from more fundamental matters. In addition, they generally ignore the intentions of the two men as either irrelevant or, at any rate, of limited importance. What matters, they argue, is not what people said (which may be misleading) or what they wanted to do (which may be uncertain) but what they actually did do. Words and motives are quicksands, according to this view, while history should be based squarely on the rock of deeds.

There are indeed many similarities between Gladstone and Disraeli. Neither was prepared to devote much time to foreign affairs, having other concerns in government, and yet both would have liked to dominate Europe - Disraeli for prestige, Gladstone because he always thought he knew best. Even on the issue of the Concert of Europe, there is little between them. Disraeli may have spoken fewer languages than Gladstone and evinced no positive enthusiasm for international conferences, but he did use Concert machinery, and on one occasion - at Berlin - he used it far more successfully than Gladstone ever did. On the Eastern Question, also, differences which at one time seemed great now seem far less important. At the Congress of Berlin, the Conservative leader agreed that a Bulgarian state should be set up, as Gladstone had demanded in his 1876 pamphlet on the Bulgarian massacre, and neither of them approved the 'Big Bulgaria' of the treaty of San Stefano. In office after 1880 Gladstone did nothing of any substance to encourage self-determination in the Balkans. Nor did he dispose of Cyprus, the spoils of the Congress which he had complained about while in opposition. And if taking Cyprus was aggressive and immoral, so too was the invasion of Egypt, another example of the strong seizing the territory of the weak. (After the invasion in 1882 a critic said he could hear 'a hollow and ghostlike laugh of derision' from Disraeli's grave, while Bright considered Gladstone's action 'simply damnable - worse than anything ever perpetrated by Dizzie'.) Is there really much to choose between the actions of the two premiers on this score? Why should one be called an imperialist and the other an anti-imperialist, when more territory was gained for the British Empire by the latter? And can it really be argued that Disraeli was more reckless and aggressive in his foreign policy? Admittedly the Conservative risked war against Russia in 1877-8, but so did Gladstone after the Penjdeh incident in 1885. Should we, perhaps, write of 'Gladraeli-ism', to emphasise the essential similarities of the two men in foreign policy?

However, it is quite possible to argue that neither the traditional nor the modern viewpoint is really adequate. They are both simple - and perhaps simplistic - interpretations, whereas arguably comparing Gladstone and Disraeli is a highly complex undertaking. There are several reasons for this:

i) First, there is the perennial problem of historical interpretation. The ideal is to draw interpretations from an impartial survey of all the evidence, but Gladstone and Disraeli were in office for so long, and were involved with so many important policies and events, that the surviving evidence is uncomfortably vast. It is therefore very easy to fall into the trap of forming a preconceived interpretation and then selecting evidence in order to fit in with it. Furthermore, however voluminous the evidence, there are always gaps, requiring the historian to make informed guesses. In short, the nature of historical study almost always leaves room for uncertainty.

ii) Also important is the obvious fact that Gladstone and Disraeli were not in office at the same time and under the same circumstances; and after an election, when the two changed places, the situation the new premier faced was often different in important ways from that which had confronted his predecessor. Hence it is not possible to compare their actions *scientifically* because we are not comparing like with like: the two men did not have the same weapons at their disposal in tackling the same opponents. To use a popular sporting metaphor, they did not each have a 'level playing field'. Hence the only way to construct some sort of direct comparison is to consider the hypothetical cases of what Gladstone would have done had he been in office, instead of Disraeli, in 1874-80, and of how Disraeli would have reacted had he been prime minister instead of Gladstone, especially in the key 1880-5 period. For the former we at least have Gladstone's outspoken criticisms whilst in opposition, though these certainly do not constitute proof of the policies he would have pursued in office; but for the latter, Disraeli's death in 1881 is a major obstacle. Arguably Disraeli might, for instance, have pressed for a much more active policy in the Sudan. And might he not have reacted less magnanimously than Gladstone to Britain's defeat by the Boers at Majuba Hill in 1881? This would certainly have been 'in character'. Clearly, therefore, a comparison on these lines involves insight into the minds of Gladstone and Disraeli and into their motives. To say that motives are important is not to deny that 'actions speak louder than words'; but it is to insist that history is more than merely a catalogue of events. To provide as complete a picture as possible, historians must get to grips with the minds of historical characters. Yet it remains true that hypothetical comparisons can never yield definite results and so always leave room for contrasting opinions.

iii) There are other factors as well which make a comparison between Gladstone and Disraeli difficult. Neither man could fully control either his cabinet or the 'men on the spot' whose initiatives were so vital to the turn of events. (Should we even speak of *Gladstone's* or *Disraeli's* foreign policy at all when each supplied only one element in a complex amalgam of factors?) Disraeli was held back by Derby, Gladstone by Granville; Disraeli had his uncontrollable Lord Lytton, Gladstone his General Gordon. However, this is not to say that uncontrollable elements had the same importance for each premier.

Of course the complexity involved in comparing the foreign policies of the two men should not prevent the attempt being made. Indeed the very difficulty of the exercise has its attractions: it means that the issue is not a 'closed' one, where the questions have been definitively answered or 'solved'. There can thus be a wide variety of viewpoints, all of which must be debated and criticised, and none of which should ever be tamely accepted.

b) Gladstone's Foreign Policy: Success and Failure

We have seen that Gladstone's was a very varied foreign policy, involving complex combinations of change and continuity. But is it possible to judge whether, overall, it was a success or a failure?

This seemingly simple question is in reality very complicated, for there are no agreed criteria to distinguish success from failure. Indeed the difference between them is largely a matter of interpretation. For instance, the invasion of Egypt in 1882, which to radicals was a flagrant example of Gladstone's failures (in that a costly invasion was mounted against right-minded nationalists) was, to Whigs, one of his greatest successes (in that the action overcame rebel forces and protected British interests).

There are as many criteria by which to evaluate success or failure as there are people to formulate them. However, there are several widely employed criteria. One is that success in foreign policy depends on the degree to which national interests are fostered. On this score, Gladstone's policies certainly exhibited some success. This can be seen, for instance, in Afghanistan and South Africa. In Afghanistan, which was perceived as a vital buffer state protecting India, neither Britain nor Russia achieved dominance. Gladstone risked war in 1885 and the Russians temporarily backed off. Honours were perhaps even. In South Africa too it would be unwise to describe the Liberals' achievements as either total success or total failure, partly because Britain's national interests in this area were uncertain. But at least bloodshed was largely avoided: the first Boer War was nothing like as violent as the second, in 1899-1902, when the Conservatives were in power.

Evaluations based on the criterion of national interests are unlikely to produce uniform judgements, since individuals will vary in deciding what really benefits the nation. A simpler criterion for judging success and failure is whether Gladstone fulfilled his aims or not. Here we seem to be on firmer ground, and we can say categorically that he certainly failed in his aim to get the Concert system to function effectively. In June 1885, after five continuous years of Gladstone's Liberal administration, his successor, Lord Salisbury, remarked that the Liberals had at last 'achieved their long desired "Concert of Europe". They have succeeded in uniting the continent of Europe - against England'. France had been alienated by the invasion of Egypt, Russia by the tussle over Afghanistan, and Bismarck's Germany was hostile. In addition, Austria, alarmed at Gladstone's anti-Turkish views, was firmly under Germany's wing, as was Italy. Gladstone had been beaten by Bismarck's *realpolitik*. But should Gladstone's efforts in this sphere be written off as a complete and abject failure?

Perhaps there is something to be said in mitigation. After all, Europe lived to regret its favouring of Bismarck over Gladstone. The German Chancellor may have kept the peace while he was in office, but his combination of secret diplomacy and military preparedness paved the way for troubles in the future. Perhaps co-operation and conciliation, rather than competition and suspicion, might have served Europe better. Gladstone had predicted that the harsh Treaty of Frankfurt of 1871 (with its 'violent laceration' of Alsace and Lorraine from France), and thereafter competitive nationalism, would have fatal consequences. Some might say, therefore, that he had been right all along and that his inability to revive the Concert was at least a gallant failure. In reaching this conclusion they would be rejecting as unduly narrow the view that the 'fulfilment of aims' is the *sole* criterion for success. Many would insist that real success or failure must be judged not only in relation to aims, and their fulfilment or non-fulfilment, but in relation to morality. For instance, a murderer who efficiently slaughtered his victims might well be adjudged to have accomplished his aims successfully, but he is hardly likely to be considered a 'success' in more general terms by those who respect human life.

Therefore we need to try to formulate a judgement which takes account of the 'aims' criterion and the 'morality' criterion. This should be possible for Gladstone, since his definition of success hinged on the issue of morality. In short, his major aim was to act morally. He gave little emphasis to the 'national advantage' criterion, believing that Britain had no special rights and that its interests should not be selfishly elevated above those of the rest of mankind.

To what degree did Gladstone adhere to his moral principles, especially those espoused in Midlothian? Conversely, to what degree were his actions dictated by pragmatism or expediency? In short, was he sincere or a humbug? First, it is worth considering Gladstone's own answer to this question. Perhaps, as some historians suspect, he knew in his heart that he had sometimes done wrong, for instance, by invading Egypt. Yet publicly he always insisted that he had acted in a way that was morally correct. In 1885 he wrote to John Bright insisting that, though his government had resorted to force on several occasions, it had done so only because honourable obligations had to be fulfilled and because of righteous purposes. Whether acting in a truly moral way or not, he was certainly never at a loss for a moral justification for his actions.

Gladstone, like many other Victorians, often spoke of morality in black-and-white terms. He refused to admit the existence of moral shades of grey or to draw up any hierarchy of moral rights and wrongs. Hence, because his governments were rarely confronted with clear-cut, right-or-wrong issues, it is impossible to judge him by his own moral rules. Often he and his ministers had to choose between courses of action which could all be justified in some way, or between policies none of which seemed morally correct. For instance, the invasion of Egypt, while ignoring the rights of Egyptians to choose their own government, did fulfil British promises to the Khedive and did restore law and order. Therefore the invasion could be considered moral, as the alternative of standing aside and taking no action also could be seen. Similarly, the London Convention and the annexation of Bechuanaland, while resting on force rather than agreement, could be justified on humanitarian grounds in that the local population would benefit far more from British rather than Boer administration. This, to some, seemed a good moral case of the 'ends justifying the means'. To annex Bechuanaland might break one moral rule, in that it deprived local people of their right to govern themselves, and yet it fulfilled another, in that it had morally beneficial results, while to take no action, and watch the Boers expand westwards, might be considered a more culpable 'sin of omission'. On the other hand, there were times when no moral option seemed to exist. To foster Egyptian claims to the Sudan seemed immoral to Gladstone, and yet to ignore them meant that the Khedive's regime would become even weaker, thus necessitating an immoral lengthening of Britain's presence in Egypt.

It is impossible for historians to give a definitive verdict on the morality of Gladstone's foreign policies. It is very tempting, of course, to condemn him as a humbug: the exaggerated moral criticisms against Disraeli, made during the Midlothian campaign, might with some poetic justice be used against Gladstone himself. Yet circumstances do alter cases, and it would be unjust to condemn Gladstone for actions which, to some extent, were forced upon him. The 'men on the spot' obeyed his instructions no more faithfully than they had Disraeli's, and the Liberal Prime Minister could not always control his own cabinet. It is probable that Gladstone's moral record is a mixed one, in that morality and pragmatism were both important elements in his foreign policy. To attempt to formulate a more precise moral verdict is likely to be as fruitless as it would be philosophically involved. In addition, most historians are chary of making moral judgements, so complex are the issues involved in the 'moral maze'. As a result, no one is likely to be able to formulate a clear-cut conclusion acceptable to all. Perhaps therefore, instead of talking in the singular of the 'success or failure' of Gladstone's foreign policy, as though a clear-cut verdict were even theoretically possible, we might more profitably consider the 'successes and failures' of his foreign policies.

Making notes on *'The Foreign Policy of Gladstone, 1880-94'*

This is an important chapter, and hence your notes should be correspondingly detailed. The headings and sub-headings should enable you to organise your notes effectively. Pay particular attention to the concluding section: here is an opportunity for you to reach your own verdict, especially on the issue of Gladstone's success or failure. When doing this go through your notes on earlier sections of the chapter and try to judge which issues and incidents should be described as 'successes' and which as 'failures'. This exercise should help you to realise the complexity of using these seemingly simple labels. It may, at first sight, seem rather irksome to be constantly thinking about the criteria on which judgements are based, but you should soon realise that this is indispensable to real understanding.

Answering essay questions on *'The Foreign Policy of Gladstone, 1880-94'*

Questions can centre either on Gladstone's foreign policy or can range more widely, bringing in Disraeli as well as Gladstone. Consider the following:

1   How far was Gladstone a 'reluctant imperialist' in his second administration, 1880-85?
2   Explain and illustrate the chief features of Gladstone's foreign policy (excluding Ireland).
3   How fundamentally did Gladstone and Disraeli pursue contrasting foreign policies?

4 Compare Gladstone and Disraeli in their foreign policies. What measure of success did each achieve?

5 How important was the Eastern Question in British foreign policy between 1865 and 1890?

Question 2 should pose few difficulties, once you have defined the 'chief features' of his foreign policies. All the other questions, except the first part of number 4, fall into the 'quantitative' category, discussed at the end of the previous chapter.

Question 1 is straightforward. First you must pinpoint the relevant policies in the period from 1880 to 1885. Which will you select besides the obvious ones (the invasion of Egypt, South Africa and Afghanistan)? Note that the Sudan is relevant here. Next you must define the terms,

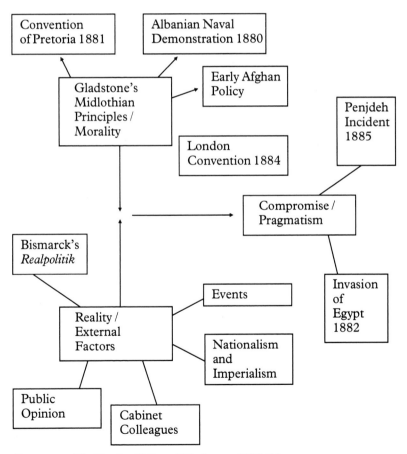

Summary - The Foreign Policy of Gladstone, 1880-94

especially 'reluctant imperialist'. How would you define 'imperialist'? Perhaps as 'expansionist' or 'aggressor'? But this is clearly a question not so much about what Gladstone did, though his actions are important, but about why he did it. Thirdly, what overall interpretation might you give? Might this be one of the occasions where you are tempted to give an 'extreme' answer and insist that the term 'reluctant imperialist' fits Gladstone 100 per cent? Consider, for instance, his policy towards Egypt. He was definitely an imperialist, because he authorised the invasion in August 1882, and he was certainly very reluctant to take this course of action. But were his expansionist actions elsewhere equally reluctant? What of his reactions to the Penjdeh incident in 1885? Did he show much hesitation here? This might be a key point, so long as, by your earlier definition of imperialism, you have decided that the incident is relevant. Be careful to devise a generalisation which takes account of all the information you are going to include in the essay; and do not deliberately miss out key areas just to make for consistency. You will be penalised for omitting information which is generally thought to be important. If you come across 'inconvenient' facts you should either modify your argument to take account of them or, alternatively, put a 'slant' on them which minimises their importance.

Questions 3 and 4, comparing Gladstone and Disraeli, are worth attempting, at least in plan form. Go through the same routine: define the key words; break Gladstone and Disraeli's work down into manageable areas (perhaps dealing with style and aims as well as policies in different geographical areas); and devise a suitable 'formula' to express the degree of difference/similarity which fits in with the information you will include in the essay.

Question 5 is also worth tackling. Remember the relevant period (from 1865 to 1890). Is it likely that the Eastern Question would have had a uniform importance over the whole 25 years? When was this issue at its most crucial stages? What other issues were also important, and how do they rank in comparison with the Eastern Question? Remember that questions of this broad type generally involve comparisons between the importance of different factors.

Source-based questions on 'The Foreign Policy of Gladstone, 1880-94'

1 Gladstone's Midlothian Principles
Read the extracts from the speech on pages 42-3 and answer the following questions.
a) What might Gladstone have meant by 'great and worthy occasions' (line 4)? (2 marks)
b) Consider the third principle. Was Gladstone being realistic in his belief that the Great Powers of Europe could be united only by issues 'connected with the common good of them all'? (3 marks)

c) Do the six principles complement each other, or might some of them conflict? Explain your answer. (5 marks)

2 'A Terrible Threat!'

Study the cartoon from *Punch* on page 51 and answer the following questions.
a) Explain how this visual depiction of Gladstone reinforces the words attributed to him. (4 marks)
b) What image of the Boers is created by the man illustrated here? (2 marks)
c) Do you agree that the criticism embodied by the cartoon amounts to no more than gentle mockery? Explain your answer. (4 marks)

3 'Gladstone Invading Egypt'

Study the cartoon on page 54 and answer the following questions.
a) What essential message is the cartoon putting across about the nature of the invasion? (3 marks)
b) Explain the ways in which this depiction of Gladstone reinforces this message. (3 marks)
c) How convincing do you find this historical interpretation? Explain your answer. (4 marks)

4 Gladstone on policy in Egypt and the Sudan

Read the extract from the speech on page 58 and answer the following questions.
a) What were the main 'difficulties of the case' (line 1) which Gladstone found so unprecedented? (2 marks)
b) Why did Gladstone think that what had been done was not 'necessarily right' (line 5) and that there had been 'possibly want of judgment' (line 10)? (3 marks)
c) Was Gladstone apologising for his actions or not? Why is it so hard to judge? (5 marks)

CHAPTER 4

'Splendid Isolation' and its Demise, 1885-1907

1 Lord Salisbury and Foreign Policy

In 1885 Lord Salisbury (then aged 55) took control of Britain's foreign policy; he dominated it for the rest of the century. He was Prime Minister from 1885 to 1892, except for a few months in 1886, and, after a short return to Liberal administration under Gladstone and then Rosebery, again from 1895 to 1902. Having already served as foreign secretary, he was extremely knowledgeable about foreign affairs, far more than either Gladstone or Disraeli had been. Indeed, such was his expertise that he doubled up as his own foreign secretary until 1900. A deeply reserved man, he usually worked in lonely isolation, rarely visiting the Foreign Office before lunch and sometimes staying away from Whitehall for a week at a time. Although he used the expert knowledge of his officials, he allowed them no part in decision-making. Yet he was no more a dictator of foreign policy than his predecessors had been. His cabinet was to influence him on several occasions, especially as his grasp of affairs seemed to falter around the turn of the century.

Salisbury was in many ways a remarkable character. He was highly intelligent, with a ready wit and an ability to express himself very pithily. Despite a reputation for eccentricity, and an appalling memory for faces, he seemed solid and dependable. He was also an amateur scientist, whose residence, Hatfield House, became the first private home in England to be lit by electricity. (He also once succeeded in electrifying its lawns!) Like Gladstone, he was a convinced Christian, but, apart from giving him an abhorrence of war, his religious beliefs did not influence his diplomacy. Unlike Gladstone, he was certainly not a moralist; and indeed some thought him a cynic. Nor, unlike Disraeli, was he particularly concerned with British prestige. Instead he was motivated by what he considered to be a sober, hard-headed appraisal of Britain's national interests. In this he had much in common with Bismarck, the German Chancellor until 1890, who practised *realpolitik*. Salisbury believed that every problem in foreign affairs should be looked at on its merits, from the point of view of national interests, so that there should be no automatic continuing of past policies. Thus open-mindedness was, to him, a virtue.

Temperamentally he was undoubtedly conservative: he would have liked things to stay as they were, since he realised that for Britain - a 'satisfied' power with a large empire - any change was likely to make things worse. Unlike most Victorians, the new Prime Minister did not believe in progress. He wrote in 1887 that, 'Whatever happens will be for the worse and therefore it is in our interests that as little should happen as possible'. In many ways he was a profoundly gloomy man. He disliked, for instance, new-fangled ideas of democracy, including the extension of the franchise to more and more people. Good government, he believed, would never come from merely counting heads. In addition, he feared for the future of Britain in the world. Yet he knew that the tide of change could not be stopped: all he could do was to try to limit change. He thus needed to be skilled in what today would be called 'damage limitation'.

a) Sources of Change

The period from the 1880s to the end of the century saw important and extensive changes in world politics. For a temperamental conservative like Salisbury such headlong change must have seemed most unwelcome, and to someone of his pessimistic outlook the days of Britain's wealth and power must have seemed numbered. As premier he had to tackle problems in several important areas:

i) There was a tremendous growth of competitive nationalism among the European powers, resulting in imperial expansion. Africa was being partitioned and China seemed likely to be divided next. The chances of Europeans coming to blows among themselves during this process seemed high, and the risks for Britain were particularly great. The fact that her colonies were so numerous and so scattered around the globe multiplied the potential for clashes with imperial rivals. The prospect of war in several places at the same time was Salisbury's nightmare scenario.

ii) Russian expansion was a consistent threat in several theatres. As always, India seemed vulnerable, and therefore it was necessary for Britain to try to stem Russian influence in its border states, especially Afghanistan and Persia (modern Iran). A Russian seizure of the Straits between the Black and Mediterranean Seas - which might result from, or precipitate, the final break-up of the Ottoman Empire - was perceived to be against British interests. It might put the route to India in jeopardy, and it would certainly lower British prestige, and thus her security, in India. Furthermore, Russian expansion into China might well harm British commercial interests there. Adding to this uncertainty were the ambitions of the newly emergent Japan in the Far East.

iii) Among the European powers, Germany was clearly the strongest economic and military power. Britain felt suspicious of Bismarck's diplomatic aims, especially since his formation of alliances left her relatively isolated. But a much greater threat was posed by his successors after 1890, especially Kaiser Wilhelm II. Might Britain need to join with Germany or, alternatively, to join a coalition against her? Neither option was without its risks, though for a time the hostility of Russia and of France - still not reconciled to British control of Egypt - made the former option seem the more attractive.

b) 'Splendid Isolation'?

Coming to office in 1885 in succession to Gladstone, Salisbury deplored the fact that Britain was isolated from the other European powers (see page 64). Yet, paradoxically, he is usually associated with the judgement that isolation was much the best policy for Britain, and that indeed it was positively 'splendid'. In fact, he has been quite erroneously associated with this view.

The phrase 'Splendid Isolation' was first used in 1896 by a member of the Canadian Parliament, who approved of Britain's refusal to become entangled in European alliances, and it was popularised in the British press. But Salisbury never used it and certainly did not approve of it. If Britain had to be isolated, it was, perhaps, as well to pretend that it was from choice, but he believed that foreign policy should be founded on realities not bluff, and he knew that isolation - unless, that is, every other Power were isolated as well - carried too many dangers. To his mind, isolation was a foolish policy not a splendid one, and he saw the need to intervene extensively in European affairs in order to protect British interests. On the other hand, he judged that membership of a long-term alliance was equally unwise since it might well serve to drag Britain into troublesome conflicts. Britain had land frontiers with all the European Powers, not in Europe but in the Empire, and it would be difficult to overcome colonial conflicts if Britain were tied to any binding alliance which limited her freedom of action. In addition, he insisted that alliances were of very limited value because future governments might repudiate them. In short, Salisbury did not want isolation and yet neither did he want an alliance. Instead he wanted co-operation with other Powers without commitment to them. Only from this position could Britain pursue the flexible policies which her national interests demanded. He therefore decided to walk a tightrope, balancing carefully between the two pitfalls of isolation and alliance. Clearly, he would need to show skill and fine judgement in foreign policy.

2 Salisbury's Policies, 1885-92

a) The Bulgarian Crisis

Salisbury immediately set about overcoming the isolation which Gladstone's foreign policy had brought about. Luckily the Russians backed down over Afghanistan (see page 48), but the new Prime Minister considered that this provided Britain with no more than a breathing space. He was still concerned about longer-term Russian expansion and about the security of India. He was also aware that France was still unreconciled to Britain's invasion of Egypt in 1882. As a result of these fears, he set about improving relations with Germany and Austria, with whom he had worked harmoniously at the Congress of Berlin in 1878.

European diplomacy around this time was dominated by Bismarck's alliances, including the Austro-German alliance of 1879, the *Dreikaiserbund* (the League of Three Emperors of Germany, Austria and Russia) of 1881, and the Triple Alliance (of Germany, Austria and Italy) of 1882. By this system Bismarck ensured his aim of peace in Europe: he had isolated France (still smarting from her defeat in the war of 1870-1) and had brought together the potentially hostile Powers of Russia and Austria, which seemed to have opposing interests in the Balkans. Both Vienna and St Petersburg were open to his moderating influence. The aim of these alliances was undoubtedly defensive, and yet their precise terms were secret and, therefore, the subject of speculation among those not included in them. They tended to create an atmosphere of fear and suspicion in Europe.

A majority of the Great Powers was allied in Bismarck's diplomatic system, and so the peace of Europe seemed secured. But what role was there for Britain, besides the existing one of insecurity, vulnerability and limited influence? Could Salisbury find a way of promoting British interests without joining an alliance?

Almost immediately a crisis erupted - in the most explosive and uncertain area of Europe, the Balkans - which allowed him to intervene. In 1885 there was a rebellion in Eastern Roumelia, part of the 'Big Bulgaria' of the short-lived treaty of San Stefano, which had been returned to Turkish rule in 1878 (see page 27). This province now demanded union with Bulgaria. Bulgarian nationalists had never accepted partition at the Congress of Berlin; and yet every other Power wished to reassert the status quo. The Turks insisted that Eastern Roumelia belonged to them, and they received the backing of the *Dreikaiserbund.* It was at this point that Salisbury became involved. He argued that, since the Turks were unable to control the area, it was best to allow it to join Bulgaria. Privately he wrote that Turkey's inability to stamp out the rebellion showed that it was 'dead'. He had a further motive: there were definite signs that the Bulgarians were stoutly anti-Russian, and so he much approved of a larger Bulgaria which would be even more capable of stemming Russian advances. Urging that Bulgaria and Eastern Roumelia should be united by a 'personal union' of the monarch, Alexander, he was standing out against a general Concert of Europe policy, much as Disraeli had done in 1876 (see page 18). Salisbury won Austria round to his way of thinking, and soon his advice was taken. It seemed, at one point, as though Russia might respond by invading Bulgaria, but Britain and Austria decided to act together to deter any such aggression. In fact, the Russians soon kidnapped Alexander, and then forced him to abdicate, but his successor proved equally anti-Russian. The main diplomatic result of this complex episode was that, since Russia and Austria found themselves on opposite sides, the League of Three Emperors came to an abrupt end. So did Britain's isolation in Europe.

b) The Mediterranean Agreements

The Triple Alliance continued to exist; and Salisbury, while not wishing to join, did want to establish good relations with its members. Already friendly with Austria, he now moved much closer to Italy. The Italians' main strategic aim was to get help in their rivalry with France in the Mediterranean and North Africa, and the German Chancellor encouraged Britain to give such support in return for Italian support against the French in Egypt. In 1887 the first 'Mediterranean Agreement' was signed. By this, Britain and Italy formed a loose coalition - not an alliance - pledged to preserve the status quo in the Mediterranean region. Salisbury assured the Queen that the compact would be to Britain's advantage, and in doing so revealed much of the basis of his thinking:

1 The English despatch ... is so drawn as to leave entirely unfettered the discretion of your Majesty's Government, as to whether, in any particular case, they will carry their support of Italy as far as 'material co-operation' ... It is as close an alliance as the
5 Parliamentary character of our institutions will permit. Your Majesty's advisers recommend it on the whole as necessary in order to avoid serious danger. If, in the present grouping of nations, which Prince Bismarck tells us is now taking place, England was left out in isolation, it might well happen that our
10 adversaries, who are coming against each other on the Continent, might treat the English Empire as divisible booty, by which their differences might be adjusted; and, though England could defend herself, it would be at fearful risk, and cost. The interests of Italy are so closely parallel to our own that we can combine with her
15 safely.

Soon Austria joined as well, and at the end of 1887 a second Agreement covered the Straits and Bulgaria. Bismarck was pleased by this arrangement. Indeed British relations with Germany improved substantially, Bismarck much preferring Salisbury to Gladstone and now referring to Britain as an 'old traditional ally'. The German Chancellor had, earlier the same year, signed a Reinsurance Treaty with Russia which, to some extent, compensated for the ending of the Three Emperors' League: Austria and Russia were no longer in alliance with each other, but at least Germany provided a link between them by way of this new treaty and his existing 1879 Austro-German alliance. Bismarck wished to influence both these allies and to dissuade them from provocative actions against each other, and yet in order to entice Russia into alliance he had found it necessary to let it be known, unofficially, that he had 'absolutely nothing against Russia going as far as Constantinople and taking the Dardanelles'. Bismarck was undoubtedly playing a dangerous game. Although wishing to prevent war, he might in fact be hastening one. However, the extension of the Mediterranean Agreements pulled his chestnuts out of the fire. This new guarantee of Turkey could be used as additional ammunition to persuade Russia to be circumspect.

So far all had gone well for Salisbury. The *Dreikaiserbund* had ended, much to his relief, and he had achieved a friendly association with the Triple Alliance. In addition, the Mediterranean Agreements meant that Russia was far less likely to take provocative action at the Straits or indeed in territory bordering India. However, Salisbury did not want a binding alliance. He turned down offers from Italy and also from Germany. Bismarck put out feelers for an alliance in 1889, but the British Prime Minister responded that it was best 'to leave the matter on the table for the time being ... without saying yes or no'. A real commitment to Germany would certainly end British isolation in Europe, but on the other hand it would compromise Britain's freedom of action. Reasoning that so long as Britain was on bad terms with France and Russia, she would always be dependent on Germany, Salisbury tried to achieve better relations with the French. In 1887 a convention was negotiated with the Sultan, whereby Britain undertook to evacuate Egypt after three years, providing her right to reoccupy the country - in order to protect the Suez Canal - was recognised. This was, in many ways, a reasonable compromise, but France, under pressure from Russia, encouraged the Sultan to resist the deal. The French hoped to secure an alliance with Russia - so that Germany would then be presented with enemies to east and west - and had therefore acquiesced in Russian wishes.

c) The Royal Navy

After a few years of Salisbury's diplomacy Britain seemed much more secure than it had been in 1885. The Prime Minister revelled in the complexities of international politics, and he used his influence to enhance Britain's bargaining power and prevent coalitions among possible enemies. Yet France had not been conciliated, the wrangle over the Egyptian invasion still continuing. Also worrying was the fact that French relations with Russia were improving, so that a Franco-Russian alliance was on the cards. In particular, the navies of France and Russia worried Salisbury. He therefore put in hand an expensive improvement of British naval defences. By the Naval Defence Act of 1889, Britain adopted the 'two power standard': the Royal Navy would henceforth be as large as the next two navies combined. This was an expensive undertaking but one which Salisbury believed the country could afford. (So did the Liberals: Gladstone tried to reject the policy when he was back in power from 1892 to 1894, but he was overridden by his party.) Only a larger British navy would allow Britain to feel secure in a potentially hostile world and avoid the need to rely on any continental ally. It would complement Salisbury's policy of being associated with the Triple Alliance, without making it a quadruple alignment.

3 Salisbury's Policies, 1895-1902

During his second long period as Prime Minister, in 1895-1902, Salisbury's worst forebodings seemed to be coming true, and he was presented with problems aplenty. He presided over foreign policy at a time not only of imperial expansion but, generally, of great turbulence in international affairs.

a) The Eastern Question

Salisbury had no affection for the Turkish Sultan, Abdul Hamid, who by the 1890s was suffering from extreme paranoid delusions, seeing spies everywhere and even refusing to sleep in the same room twice. Emotionally, Salisbury had much sympathy with the judgement that the Turks should pull out of Europe bag and baggage, and he had successfully urged that Eastern Roumelia should be allowed to quit the Empire and join Bulgaria. Yet he persisted with the traditional policy of supporting the Ottoman Empire. If this Empire collapsed, he judged, the Russians might advance to the Straits, and if Britain then failed to take retaliatory action, she would suffer a massive blow to her influence abroad. Britain's standing in India, which depended so much on prestige, would undoubtedly be harmed. The best policy, therefore, seemed to be to preserve the status quo. However, in 1895 a crisis blew up in Turkey.

There were at this time around one million Armenians in the Ottoman Empire, spread out over various provinces. They had long been oppressed; and now, amid signs of a growing national identity among them, which the Sultan found unwelcome, a slaughter began. The European ambassadors in Constantinople saw Armenians dragged onto the streets and clubbed to death. They reacted swiftly, insisting that the Sultan must mend his ways, and the massacres stopped, though only temporarily. A few weeks later they were renewed, though in Asia Minor - away from the glare of publicity - rather than in the Turkish capital. It seemed like the Bulgarian Horrors all over again, only worse, and Gladstone once more sought to orchestrate outraged British public opinion. Salisbury had therefore to appease the public by pursuing an anti-Turkish policy and doing what he could to prevent further Armenian suffering, and yet at the same time he had also to try to safeguard British interests in the area. In particular he had to dissuade the Russians from cashing in on the chaos and seizing the Straits and Constantinople.

Salisbury wished to take a very firm line. He proposed sending the British fleet to the Straits to deter the Russians. Quite clearly, he still believed in the need to defend Constantinople. Yet his cabinet, on advice from the Admiralty, was against this measure, fearing that the Royal Navy would be unable to force a passage through the Straits to attack the 'soft underbelly' of Russia and, furthermore, that Britain would come off worse if it came to war. Hence Salisbury had to content himself with hoping that the Russians would act circumspectly and with urging united action by the Powers to coerce Turkey. But the Prime Minister urged in vain, and no multilateral action was accepted. Indeed the following year, 1896, saw the troubles flaring up again. Armenians terrorists seized a bank in Constantinople, and this was the pretext for a reign of terror from the imperial forces, as for several days the Sultan's men massacred hundreds of Armenian men, women and children. Again Salisbury urged that a revived Concert of Europe should insist that the Sultan reform his administration. Otherwise - the Prime Minister advised the young Tsar Nicholas II, who was visiting Britain in September - Abdul Hamid should be deposed. Better this, and some sort of international control of the Ottoman Empire and of the Straits, than continued massacres and, sooner or later, complete anarchy in Turkey and untold consequences for Europe. But the Tsar would not agree. He insisted that the Muslims in the Ottoman Empire were remarkably loyal to the Sultan and that, in consequence, international administration would meet with fearsome opposition. Perhaps he preferred to leave the Sultan in control of the Straits until the Russians felt powerful enough to seize them. Dismayed, Salisbury had to fall back on further appeals for multilateral action, but again without success.

No aid was forthcoming for the Armenians. Only the Greeks took direct action, as part of their campaign to free all Greeks from Turkish rule: they declared war on Turkey early in 1897, but their campaigns went very badly, and Britain and other European powers had to insist that the terms imposed by the Sultan were not harsh. The Greeks had reason to thank Salisbury, but he had achieved little success in this area. The Sick Man of Europe was clinging to life with far more tenacity than the British Prime Minister had expected. It was lucky for him that British public opinion soon became more concerned with events in South Africa and Venezuela than with those in Asia Minor.

b) Diplomatic Realignment

The main result of this Ottoman crisis was a realignment in European diplomacy. Salisbury's decided that Constantinople should no longer be a focus for British strategic thinking, and this led to a breach in the Anglo-Austrian entente. The Austrians wished to extend the Mediterranean Agreements to include a binding British guarantee to defend Constantinople, but Salisbury preferred the old informal arrangements and so refused. As a result, the Mediterranean Agreements lapsed in 1897. Salisbury's policy of limited association with the Triple Alliance thus came to an end. Instead it was Germany, already giving military advice to the Sultan, which emerged as Turkey's champion. British relations with Germany were also deteriorating, especially since, following Bismarck's fall from office in 1890, the young Kaiser, Wilhelm II, began to pursue an erratic course in his foreign policy. Almost immediately he had turned down a Russian offer of renewing the Reinsurance Treaty: and this, while pleasing the British, who were anti-Russian, allowed the French to step in and secure an alliance with the Tsar in 1894. The stability which Bismarck had provided in European affairs was fast disappearing, with a consequent multiplication of problems for Europe's politicians, including Salisbury.

c) Egypt and the Nile

With the tacit abandonment of the Straits, it now seemed sensible to concentrate on building up the British presence in Egypt. From here British forces would be able to tackle the Russians, if they proceeded through the Straits. But the new position assigned to Egypt made the neighbouring Sudan more vital than ever before for Britain. Egypt had to be made secure, and so in March 1896 British forces began the conquest of the Sudan. Gordon was belatedly to be revenged, and in 1898 Kitchener won a decisive victory over the Dervishes at Omdurman. A mere 48 of his men were killed, while superior British weaponry resulted in the slaughter of about 12,000 of the Mahdi's men.

Salisbury had negotiated a series of boundary agreements in 1890-1 with other Powers to prevent friction in much of Africa and, as a result, the partition proceeded quickly and smoothly. But the struggle for control of the Upper Nile was not so easily decided. Shortly after the battle of Omdurman, British troops encountered at Fashoda a small French force which had arrived after an eighteen month march across the continent from the west coast. The French claimed the area by right of prior conquest. Conflict, which had been brewing for some time between these two rival claimants to the Upper Nile, looked distinctly possible. Who owned the region legally? No one really knew. The key issue was therefore which side would stand its ground and which withdraw. The British cabinet, against Salisbury's advice, insisted that they would not even discuss the matter until the French withdrew - and in the end they did so. France was effectively isolated, since its ally Russia was heavily involved in Manchuria, and could not risk fighting alone. In addition, the French navy was ill-prepared for war, and French society was sharply divided by the Dreyfus case, an infamous legal wrangle. Anglo-Egyptian control of the Sudan, and of the Upper Nile region, was thus established. The British, aware that they were in such a good position, drove a hard bargain. The French were allowed no compensation elsewhere, which would have allowed them to save face. The 'Fashoda Incident', the French foreign minister later insisted, delayed the fostering of good relations between the two countries.

d) Russia and China

Fears of Russian encroachments on India intensified, especially when it became clear, after 1895, that Britain would be unable to retaliate by passing through the Straits to bombard Russia's flank. A few years later Russia's railway communications reached the frontiers of Afghanistan, while in Persia the Russians seemed to be achieving influence over the Shah. The Viceroy of India felt menaced and so alerted Salisbury. But in fact it was in China that Russian encroachments seemed most troublesome.

Britain had commercial interests in the decaying Chinese empire, weakly ruled by the ailing Manchu dynasty, which might be jeopardised if the country were partitioned. The British therefore favoured an Open Door policy: all nations could trade with China but none annex territory. But would China, the sick man of Asia, be able to survive intact? To many it seemed unlikely. *The Times* judged that Britain's effort to prevent the partition of China was 'trying to keep the ocean out with a mop'. The omens looked especially bleak after Japan scored an easy victory in a war with China in 1894-5. Only the 'triple intervention' of Russia, France and Germany prevented the Japanese from imposing a very harsh peace settlement. Nor was Japan the only Power to seek territorial concessions. At first it had seemed that Russian interests, which were in the north, would not conflict with those of Britain, which were in the centre and south of the country, especially around Shanghai. But tension became acute. At the end of 1897 the Germans seized territory, and early the following year the Russians sent their fleet to Port Arthur, on which they soon obtained a lease. There was talk of war in the British press, but Salisbury calmed the situation, even concluding an agreement with the Russians to build a railway in northern China. Nevertheless the situation remained dangerously fluid, and in 1900 the 'Boxer Rebellion' - in which Chinese nationalists attacked Europeans - broke out in Peking in protest at domination by foreigners. But this only exacerbated the situation. The Russians used it as an excuse to send an army into Manchuria to extend their control over the region. The whole of China seemed to be teetering on the edge of anarchy.

The Europeans were undoubtedly skating on thin ice in China. Their rivalries, it seemed, might well lead to confrontation among themselves. But in the end it was this fear which made them tread warily. Instead of partitioning China, the Powers agreed on spheres of influence in which they could trade undisturbed. Russia, France, Germany and Britain came to mutually satisfactory agreements, though no one could be sure how long this truce would last.

e) USA

There were several quarrels with the United States in this period. The most serious arose in 1895-6 over a boundary dispute between the independent South American republic of Venezuela and British Guiana, which was part of the British Empire. Ostensibly this problem had nothing to do with the United States, but the Venezuelans appealed for help and the American President, Grover Cleveland, announced that he was stepping in to arrange arbitration. The United States clearly regarded both North and South America as their 'sphere of influence'. It took Salisbury four months to respond and, when he did, he refused to recognise the US government's right to intervene: he believed that Cleveland was bluffing and that the issue would soon 'fizzle away'. But the President then sent a strong note of protest. It even seemed, for a time, that a war might begin: some Americans talked of invading Canada, while Irish-Americans were quick to volunteer to fight against the detested English. The British Ambassador reported a condition of mind among the American public 'which can only be described as hysterical'. The government in London was shocked: they expected enmity from the French and the Russians but not from the Americans. British politicians undoubtedly resented this unexpectedly strong reaction, but Salisbury's government nevertheless acquiesced. The Prime Minister took the realistic decision that there was no point in risking a war with the USA, especially when there were problems in plenty elsewhere, and arbitration was accepted. It took three years before the results of this were announced, and in fact the judgements went very much in Britain's favour, but what mattered most was not this precise settlement of an obscure border region, which was mostly jungle anyway, but that Britain had accepted American dominance in this part of the world.

A few years later, Salisbury's government also agreed that the United States could construct the Panama Canal on their own, despite an earlier understanding that the British would play a part, and Royal Navy warships were withdrawn from their bases in the West Indies. In addition, Britain remained neutral, despite secret sympathies for Spain, when a Spanish-American war broke out, over control of Cuba, in 1898. By this time Anglo-American relations had vastly improved, but only at the price of diminished British influence in the world. Such unfortunate developments, Salisbury decided philosophically, had to be accepted: British power was limited and therefore commitments had to be scaled back accordingly. The Western hemisphere could not be a British priority, in view of events elsewhere.

f) The Boer War

Among the younger generation of Conservative politicians, there were many who were enthusiasts for imperial expansion. The most prominent of them was the former Radical Joseph Chamberlain, who had left the Liberals in the 1880s in protest at Gladstone's policy of Irish Home Rule. In 1895, when invited to join Salisbury's government, he showed his enthusiasm by opting for the relatively minor post of Colonial Secretary rather than seeking a more senior office of state. Far less cautious than Salisbury, he believed that Britain's huge but economically backward empire could be developed, thereby enhancing British wealth and status as a world Power and also absorbing unemployment and so preventing social troubles at home. But Salisbury himself was no mindless expansionist: he was too aware of the problems that would arise from colonial adventures and far too sceptical to be carried away by imperial dreams.

Trouble in South Africa, therefore, was not of the Prime Minister's making. Problems really stemmed from the settlers there. In the 1890s Cecil Rhodes, Prime Minister of Cape Colony, extended British influence northwards. But he did not neglect southern Africa itself, especially after valuable diamonds and gold had been discovered in the Transvaal. Even before this, rivalry had been intense between the British and the Boer settlers; but now Britons began to move into the Transvaal in ever greater numbers. The fact that they were treated poorly by Paul Kruger's government - and especially that they were denied the vote - prepared the way for even more intense troubles. In 1895 Rhodes supported an armed coup. A raid led by Dr Jameson was to coincide with a rising by the British mine workers, but in fact the latter failed to occur and Kruger's government had little trouble coping. The British government hastily denied all knowledge of Jameson's activities, though Chamberlain may well have been implicated. However, this was not the end of the problem. Britain's High Commissioner for South Africa, Alfred Milner, then put intense pressure on the Transvaal government to grant full rights to British workers. It is unlikely that he was trying to push Kruger into a full-scale war. Probably he simply wanted to bully him into submission. So did the British Cabinet, under Chamberlain's influence, and in 1899 British troops were sent to South Africa - despite Salisbury's misgivings - to add to the pressure. Yet war was the result. Kruger believed that the British were closing in on him and that his only hope was a preemptive strike. In October he launched a surprise attack on Cape Colony. The second Boer War had begun.

The British had made few preparations for war, but they expected an easy victory nevertheless. In fact they did not win until 1902, by which time 22,000 Britons had been killed, over 20,000 Boers had died in British concentration camps, and £250 million had been spent. The war was a profound shock for the British, driving home recognition of their patent weaknesses. As Kipling said, it provided 'no end of a lesson'. This climax to the partition of Africa significantly diminished British confidence and also led to the growth of anti-imperialist feeling. In addition, it profoundly altered British foreign affairs. The war helped to sour Anglo-German relations. In 1896 the Kaiser of Germany, who was already supplying the Boers with weapons, had sent a telegram congratulating Kruger on repulsing the Jameson raid, and during the war the Germans were highly critical of British policy. In particular the treatment of Boer prisoners of war was denounced as 'brutal and inhuman'. Germany observed strict neutrality during the war, and it was only the French and the Russians who talked of intervening against Britain. But a definite fillip was given to those who considered that isolation was inimical to British interests. Should Britain in fact sign a full-scale alliance? And if so, with whom?

4 The Diplomatic 'Revolution' of 1902-7

a) Failure of a German Alliance

Around the turn of the century there was an extensive and anxious debate about Britain's foreign policy. The multiplication of problems, and especially the fiasco in South Africa, convinced many politicians that Salisbury's policy of avoiding a European alliance ought to be ended. The ageing Prime Minister was indeed thought by several members of his own cabinet - not least Joseph Chamberlain - to be living in the past and to be increasingly out of touch. The death of Queen Victoria in 1901 complemented the calls for change: a new era seemed to demand new policies.

Some thought that Germany would be the best bet for an ally. This was particularly the view of Chamberlain, who had made unauthorised overtures to Germany in 1898, but it was the new Foreign Secretary, Lord Lansdowne, who opened official negotiations in 1901. In his first letter as Foreign Secretary, Lansdowne revealed a preconceived idea - 'that we should use every effort to maintain and, if we can, to strengthen the good relations which at present exist between the Queen's Government and that of the [German] Emperor'. He believed that Britain had in the past 'survived in spite of our isolation'. But whereas he wanted an Anglo-German defensive alliance, the Germans insisted that Britain should join the Triple Alliance, which was due for renewal around this time.

Might Britain finally join the Triple Alliance, despite the fact that this would tie her to the defence of central Europe? In May 1901 Lansdowne sent his Prime Minister a draft treaty. In reply, in a masterly memorandum, Salisbury argued not for 'splendid isolation' but for a 'free hand'. He wrote that the practical effect of an alliance would be,

1 (1) If England were attacked by two Powers - say France and
Russia - Germany, Austria, and Italy would come to her assistance.
(2) Conversely, if either Austria, Germany, or Italy were attacked
by France and Russia, or, if Italy were attacked by France and
5 Spain, England must come to the rescue. Even assuming that the
Powers concerned were all despotic, and could promise anything
they pleased, with a full confidence that they would be able to
perform the promise, I think it is open to much question whether
the bargain would be for our advantage. The liability of having to
10 defend the German and Austrian frontiers against Russia is heavier
than that of having to defend the British Isles against France. Even,
therefore, in its most naked aspect the bargain would be a bad one
for this country. Count Hatzfeldt [the German ambassador in
London] speaks of our 'isolation' as constituting a serious danger
15 for us. Have we ever felt that danger practically? If we had
succumbed in the revolutionary war, our fall would not have been
due to our isolation. We had many allies but they would not have
saved us if the French Emperor [Napoleon] had been able to
command the Channel. Except during his reign we have never
20 been in danger; and, therefore, it is impossible for us to judge
whether the 'isolation' under which we are supposed to suffer, does
or does not contain in it any elements of peril. It would hardly be
wise to incur novel and most onerous obligations, in order to guard
against a danger in whose existence we have no historical reason
for believing.

Many historians have interpreted these words as an argument against
any alliance; but, strictly speaking, Salisbury was merely saying that the
disadvantages of an alliance with Germany and her existing allies
outweighed the advantages. The issue of whether an alliance with
someone else might be possible was left undecided. At all events,
Salisbury had buried the idea of Britain joining the Triple Alliance.
Naval rivalry and trade rivalry with Germany (see pages 97-101) soon
meant that the proposal was not renewed.
    Even Chamberlain admitted defeat. Instead of continuing his search
for a German alliance, he now put his hope for future security on the
British Empire. In a speech in Birmingham in January 1902 he insisted
that he was

1 an imperialist, and proud of the name ... We are citizens of no
mean city. We carry civilization, British justice, British law and
Christianity to peoples who until our advent have lived in
ignorance, in bitter conflict and whose territories have fallen to us
5 to develop. We are people of a great empire ... We have the feeling,
unfortunately, that we have to count upon ourselves alone, and I
say, therefore, it is the duty of British statesmen and it is the duty of

the British people to count upon themselves alone, as their
ancestors did, yes in a splendid isolation, surrounded by our
10 kinsfolk.

His fixed idea was henceforth to be imperial unity, symbolised by free
trade within the Empire and the imposition of protective tariffs against
the rest of the world. In 1903 he left the government to campaign -
unsuccessfully - for these measures.

b) Salisbury: a Summary

Lord Salisbury left the Foreign Office in 1900 and was replaced by Lord
Lansdowne. In 1902, after the defeat of the Boers, he resigned as Prime
Minister. His health had been poor for some time, and he had been
finding it increasingly difficult to control his cabinet. Lansdowne
remained at the Foreign Office, while Arthur Balfour, Salisbury's
nephew, became Prime Minister.

How ably had Salisbury guided Britain's foreign policy since 1885?
The question is difficult to answer. He had been involved with foreign
policy for so long that, almost inevitably, his record was a mixed one. At
his death in 1903 commentators decided that Salisbury's control of
foreign affairs had been sound but unexciting: he was said to have
possessed a powerful analytical mind, but one which saw too clearly the
disadvantages of every course of action. In short, it was widely believed
that he had been too cautious. Commentators were thus repeating,
though guardedly, the criticisms levelled at him in his final years, when
one outspoken critic referred to him as 'that brilliant, obstructive
deadweight at the top'. The times seemed to call for active, positive
policies not reactive, defensive ones.

After the massive destruction of the Great War, however, such
caution as Salisbury had displayed seemed a virtue rather than a vice,
and he began to be praised for his moderation and 'intelligent inaction'.
He seemed to have handled foreign affairs better than his successors.

In more recent times, judgements on Salisbury have been varied, but
most historians have praised his calm, unruffled attempts to avoid the
perils of both isolation and commitment in foreign affairs. They have
approved his avoidance of both war and of the sort of spectacular
successes which alienated other Powers. Perhaps his greatest supporter
has been J.A.S. Grenville, who has argued that even Bismarck - let alone
Chamberlain - never got the better of him. He judges that it is his
'careful and patient handling of an immense variety of serious
international problems' that shows Salisbury's true greatness.

However, it must be said Salisbury had his failures. Quite often
colleagues took him further than he wanted to go, as with the settlement
of the Fashoda incident, and he was also unable to prevent the second
Boer War. It should also be recognised that there were problems ahead

for Britain after 1902. It is true that issues only became acute after Salisbury was out of office, but perhaps a more straightforward commitment to Europe, in the form of an alliance, might have lessened the problems Britain experienced in the years leading up to the Great War of 1914-18.

c) The Anglo-Japanese Alliance

In 1902 Britain signed an alliance with the rising eastern Power of Japan. This has generally been interpreted as a sharp break with past British policy. The *Spectator* called it the end of the 'fixed policy of not making alliances'. Certainly it shocked many commentators. Predictably, Salisbury was not keen on this departure from his past policy of avoiding such commitments, but his grip on affairs was weak. Why did Britain decide to make this alliance?

First, there was no doubt that Japan was a rising and important Power in the Far East. She had avoided the fate that was overtaking China by co-operating with the west. Ever since the American Commodore Perry had landed in Japan in 1853 and insisted that the country should be opened to western trade, the Japanese had ended their traditional policy of isolation. Instead they had aimed to produce rapid economic growth. Japan's leaders skilfully played off one western nation against another to ensure that no single Power was dominant. German advisers, for instance, helped to modernise their army, while the British helped to expand the navy. Clearly, Japan's policy of 'westernisation' included an imitation of the western nations' competitive nationalism. Japan therefore aimed to expand both its influence and its territory. It would not be content for long to be the pupil of the west: instead it hoped to be strong enough to be free of western domination. These ambitions accounted for Japan's war against China in 1894-5 and for the extreme resentment bred by the intervention of Russia, France and Germany to moderate the peace settlement Japan wished to impose on China.

The obvious next step for Japan, in its search to be recognised as an equal of the European Powers, was to form an alliance. Hitherto the alliance system had been confined to Europeans, who had traditionally lumped together non-whites as inferior. An alliance would therefore have symbolic value, as well as perhaps providing tangible benefits. Perhaps the Russians might be viable partners? Japan and Russia were rivals in China, but the Japanese considered a deal whereby Russia would be free to control Manchuria, while recognising Japan's preeminence in Korea. But the Russians turned down a deal - much to their subsequent regret. As a result, France, Russia's ally, was also ruled out. Austria had no real interests in the Far East. Therefore the choice was between Germany and Britain. In the end, Britain was the favoured partner, perhaps because so many important Japanese figures had connections, including naval training, with Britain or the English-speaking world. The key figure in influencing the decision appears to have been Hayashi, the Japanese ambassador in London, who was a convinced Anglophile. He was a leading Freemason in London, and Edward VII had awarded him the Grand Cross of the Victorian Order. Under his influence, the Japanese government in 1901 sought an alliance with Britain.

From Britain's point of view, there were several advantages to this proposal. First, it would help Britain to overcome the isolation which, with the Boer War still raging, seemed so menacing. More particularly, it would provide security against the menace of Russia. Britain felt vulnerable in the Far East, and if it came to a war with Russia - backed up by its ally France - Britain would be hard pressed indeed. The cabinet was warned towards the end of 1901 that Royal Naval vessels would soon be outnumbered by combined Franco-Russian forces in the Far East: Britain would have four battleships stationed there, while her rivals would have nine. Not surprisingly, therefore, the Admiralty was the department of state most keen to see a Japanese alliance. Ideally, the British would have liked to settle their problems direct with Russia; but Lansdowne was rebuffed by the Tsar's ministers much as the Japanese had been, and so he agreed to negotiate with Japan.

Lansdowne believed that Japan was probably not strong enough to provide real security against Russia, and he would have preferred an alliance with Germany. But it was at this point, in the middle of 1901, that Salisbury quashed the proposal (see page 82), and so an alliance with Japan was accepted as second best. A Japanese alliance - providing suitable terms could be negotiated - would at least prevent any Russo-Japanese alliance, of which the British had heard rumours, and it would also tip the odds more in Britain's favour in the Far East. What was more, it might well deter Russia from aggressive action altogether.

Hayashi conducted negotiations for Japan. When they were completed, it seemed that Lansdowne had achieved exactly the terms he needed. The alliance was to be strictly defensive, and the treaty's preamble spoke of the desire of the two countries 'to maintain the status quo in the Far East': Britain and Japan would provide mutual aid if either of them were attacked by more than one Power. Britain would therefore not have to meet a Franco-Russian combination alone.

The treaty was signed in January 1902. It seemed that Britain would have a useful ally in the Far East, and moreover would still be uncommitted and have a free hand in Europe. Here, it seemed, were all the advantages of an alliance without the corresponding disadvantages; or, conversely, all the advantages of detachment from Europe with far fewer of the attendant fears. Therefore this Japanese alliance should not be interpreted as constituting the complete break with previous foreign policy which an alliance with a European Power would have been. Instead, it was no more than a modification of traditions. Indeed, some have said that an alliance with an Eastern Power merely emphasised

Britain's distance from the other European Powers.

This is not to say that the alliance was a complete success. British diplomats made a fundamental mistake: they had assumed that the Japanese, like themselves, wanted extra security. However, in reality, the Japanese looked upon their agreement with Britain as no more than a preliminary achievement of symbolic equality, to be followed by fresh conquests. In 1904 their fleet attacked the Russian squadron at Port Arthur in China. A full-scale war then began, with the Japanese emerging as surprising but nevertheless easy victors the following year. Britain had acquired as an ally not a defensive but a distinctly aggressive Power.

d) The Anglo-French Entente

The alliance with Japan did not make a significant difference to Britain's position in Europe, and Lansdowne was determined to achieve a greater measure of security here. A breakthrough came in 1904, when Britain and France signed the *Entente Cordiale.*

Given the bitter quarrels in which Britain and France had engaged ever since 1882, this 'friendly understanding' at first sight seems entirely unexpected. It is explained by several factors. On the British side, there was a new alarm at German activities. The proposal for a German alliance had been only narrowly defeated in 1898-1901, but after this period the British government became more and more convinced that Germany was a troublesome element in European affairs. In particular the growing German navy seemed alarming (see pages 98-101). A memorandum from the Admiralty in 1902 highlighted the view that the Kaiser's fleet was 'designed for a possible conflict with the British fleet'. In view of a possible German menace, a settlement with France was obviously desirable. Secondly, a group of civil servants in the Foreign Office forcefully advocated an agreement with France as a means of lessening British reliance on Germany. Thirdly, an agreement with France would help to ensure that the Russo-Japanese war, then raging in the Far East, did not escalate to produce warfare between the allies of the combatants, namely France and Britain. Finally, an end to disputes with France had long been desired by the British. The invasion of Egypt in 1882 had originally been planned as a joint Anglo-French operation, and the friction that resulted from Britain's unilateral action had been entirely unwelcome in London (see page 55).

From the French point of view also, the time was ripe for reconciliation. Memories of the invasion of Egypt were growing dim, and rivalries over the Scramble for Africa, especially the 1898 Fashoda incident, were also now considered as past history. France's present African ambitions were centred on Morocco, where Britain had significant trading interests, and so, if possible, London's goodwill had to be secured. In addition, the French too were anxious to avoid getting dragged into the Russo-Japanese conflict. They had always seen their alliance with Russia (1894) as a means of checking the Triple Alliance (and especially Germany): they certainly did not want it to draw them into an unwelcome war with Britain and Japan, which would only cheer German hearts.

Following a state visit to Paris by the British monarch, Edward VII, which the French President reciprocated by visiting London, the agreement was signed. Several minor, but irritant, colonial disputes were settled: Siam (modern Thailand) was accepted by both sides as a buffer state, between French Indochina and British Burma; Britain abandoned claims to Madagascar; the New Hebrides were put under joint administration; and mutually acceptable fishing rights off Newfoundland were agreed. More importantly, the French finally agreed to accept British control in Egypt, while Britain recognised French predominance in Morocco.

e) The Anglo-Russian Entente

In 1907 a further entente was signed, this time by the Liberal government which had replaced the Conservatives two years earlier. It was between Britain and its other traditional rival, Russia. This new alignment, like the *Entente Cordiale,* marked a departure from previous policy; but for many years the British had wanted to settle their differences with Russia. Only then would India be really safe, while only a settlement with Russia would leave Britain really secure in Europe.

Russia's defeat by Japan in 1905, which helped to unleash an attempted revolution in St Petersburg, perhaps made the Russians more willing to settle their problems with Britain. Their vulnerability meant that they were in no position to threaten British interests, while the British were keen to cash in on a weakness which, after all, might only be temporary. Indeed, after recovery, the Russians might decide to focus their ambitions not on China, where Japan was now so powerful, but on Central Asia.

Talks began in 1906 and came to fruition in the summer of 1907. The Anglo-Russian Agreement had three sections. (i) While (hypocritically) recognising the independence of Persia, the two Powers agreed that the country should be divided into three zones of influence: a Russian zone, a British zone, and a neutral area in between. The British sphere was to be in the south of the country, constituting a buffer for India. (ii) Similarly in Afghanistan, the Russians recognised British interests in the area contiguous with India, while Britain agreed to respect the special rights of Russia along its Afghan border. (iii) Both countries agreed to recognise the independence of Tibet and promised not to interfere with its internal administration. This new entente was considered to be far from perfect, and the Viceroy of India believed that it failed to do enough to ensure real security. But, on the whole, it was undoubtedly valuable; and henceforth the defence of India ceased to be such a worrying, and dominant, consideration for the British government.

Since Britain had already signed the *Entente Cordiale* with France, the new agreement with Russia was hailed as completing the Triple Entente. To some this seemed a sensible response to the Triple Alliance of Germany, Austria and Italy; but to others it was a dangerous sign that Britain had departed from traditions and was taking sides in the division of Europe into two armed camps.

f) Conclusion: a Revolution in Diplomacy?

Many have argued that this new alignment, comprising the alliance with Japan and the ententes with France and Russia, amounted to a revolution in British foreign policy. In contrast to the 'splendid isolation' of Salisbury's days (so the argument runs), Britain had now made positive commitments which not only ended her isolation but committed her to the anti-German camp. Corroborative evidence for this interpretation came in the First World War, when Britain fought alongside France and Russia against Germany and its allies.

While much depends on the definition of 'revolution' that is accepted, some would consider this interpretation faulty in several respects. To begin with, Salisbury had not pursued 'splendid isolation' at all: he had been at pains to become involved in European affairs, as shown for instance by the Mediterranean Agreements of 1887. He had not sought isolation, he had sought association with the European Powers, while refusing to commit himself irrevocably to any particular allies. He wished to keep a free and flexible hand, so as to avoid being dragged into war by restless partners. Was this policy really so different from that pursued by his successors in 1902-7? The Japanese alliance really committed Britain to very little: Britain merely promised to help Japan if she were attacked by a coalition of Powers, a remote possibility made even more unlikely by Britain's guarantee. Similarly, the ententes were not designed to commit Britain to any action: they were a settlement of past disputes, not a guarantee for the future. Unlike most full-scale alliances, they singled out no particular enemy and involved no joint military or naval plans. They were a sign of newly developing goodwill between Britain and two former rivals. As such they gave Britain the sort of freedom of diplomatic manoeuvre which Salisbury had always desired, for the less Anglo-French and Anglo-Russian tension existed, the less did Britain need a European ally. Certainly there seemed now to be no great need for a German alliance. In fact, Britain now had a freer hand in Europe than at almost any other time.

Popular misconceptions on this issue have arisen firstly by misunderstanding Salisbury's policies and, secondly, by misinterpreting the Ententes as essentially anti-German. It is true that, in 1902-7, fear of Germany was growing and that this was a factor influencing both the

Japanese alliance and the French and Russian Ententes; but this is not to say that the Ententes, in their origins, were primarily directed against Germany. Certainly the British did not view the *Entente Cordiale* as much more than a settlement of past disputes. Worry about German ambitions existed in the background, but British diplomats wanted a freer hand in European affairs not a commitment to back up the French in their long-running enmity with Germany. Nor did the French view their Entente with Britain as relevant to Germany. French security against the Germans lay, at this time, in the Franco-Russian alliance: this alignment meant that, in any future war, Germany would have to fight on two fronts, against the French in the West and the Russians in the East. Russia was therefore considered a far more important ally than Britain could conceivably be, and the French would certainly have been far more willing to jettison Britain's friendship than Russia's alliance. Similarly, the Entente of 1907 had little relevance to Germany: Britain's overwhelming concern was with India not with the Kaiser.

It may thus be unconvincingly melodramatic to talk of any 'revolution' in British foreign policy in 1902-7. There was too much continuity with previous policy for this. The Ententes were not alliances, and they preserved Britain's 'semi-detached' position in Europe. The French, realising after Russia's ignominious defeat against Japan that their only ally was far weaker militarily than they had assumed, soon decided that they wished to transform the Entente into an anti-German alliance, but there was no guarantee that they would succeed. The future was still uncertain around 1907, and Britain was still largely uncommitted in its relations with the European Powers.

Making notes on 'Splendid Isolation' and its Demise, 1885-1907

It is very easy to treat the period 1885-1907 as a series of separate incidents, and indeed you need to have full notes on issues such as the reality or illusion of splendid isolation, the 1902 Japanese alliance and the Ententes of 1904 and 1907; but it is also worthwhile considering the period as a whole, and how far Britain's position around 1907 involved substantial change from the 1880s. Be certain, therefore, to pause when making notes on the final, concluding sub-section. Do not passively accept the interpretation put forward here. Can you substantiate a case for a revolution in diplomacy? Only if you cannot should you agree that one did not occur.

You may also wish to construct a parallel series of notes, tracing Britain's relations with each important European country separately. A chronological survey of this kind will help you to see events and developments from a different perspective, making it much easier to spot change and continuity.

For further details of the 1900-7 period, see the section in the next chapter on the deterioration on Anglo-German relations.

Answering essay questions on *'"Splendid Isolation" and its Demise, 1885-1907'*
A wide variety of questions is possible. Consider the following:

1   Explain why Britain made an alliance with Japan in 1902.
2   Why did Britain form an alliance with Japan (1902) but conclude only Ententes with France (1904) and Russia (1907).
3   'That brilliant, obstructive deadweight at the top.' Discuss the foreign policy of Lord Salisbury in the light of this comment.

Remember that for questions 1 and 2, which seem very narrow and

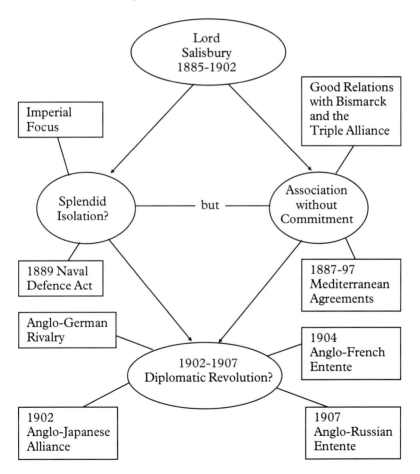

Summary - 'Splendid Isolation' and its Demise, 1885-1907

specific, you have to put the key facts into a wide context in terms of both what was happening at the same time (for instance, with Germany) and of earlier events and developments. For question 3, on the other hand, which covers a long period (1885-1902), you must refer to specific events and not confine yourself to generalities.

Two other questions are worth looking at in detail:

4   How far was 'splendid isolation' really 'splendid' in the years from 1886 to 1902?

5   To what extent is it true to say that a 'revolution' occurred in British foreign policy in the early years of the twentieth century?

You should by now be familiar with quantitative (or evaluative) questions ('how far?', 'to what extent?'). Try to construct essay plans for these titles. Remember the importance of (i) defining key terms, (ii) breaking down the question into convenient sub-divisions, and (iii) devising a direct formula in answer to 'how far?'

Source-based questions on "'Splendid Isolation" and its Demise, 1885-1907'

1 Salisbury on the first Mediterranean Agreement
Read the extract from Salisbury's letter on page 74 and answer the following questions.
a)   What did Salisbury mean by his insistence that the agreement was 'as close an alliance as the Parliamentary character of our institutions will permit' (line 4)? (2 marks)
b)   Who were the 'adversaries' (line 10) who might seek to divide the British Empire? (2 marks)
c)   Using the evidence contained in the extract, estimate how important Salisbury considered the Agreements to be. (6 marks)

2 Salisbury on joining the Triple Alliance
Read the extract from the memorandum on page 83 and answer the following questions.
a)   Explain why Salisbury cast doubts on whether the Powers would adhere to the terms of a possible alliance. (2 marks)
b)   Why was he confident of the security of Britain's position? How might critics have responded to his views? (8 marks)

3 Chamberlain on Splendid Isolation
Read the extract from the speech on page 83 and answer the following questions.
a)   From evidence in the speech, estimate how wholeheartedly Chamberlain favoured 'splendid isolation'. (5 marks)
b)   Describe the mood of the speech. (5 marks)

CHAPTER 5

Britain and the Origins of the First World War

In August 1914 Britain's Liberal government, led by Herbert Asquith, declared war on Germany and so joined what was later known as the First World War. The conflict turned out to be a titanic struggle, lasting over four years and producing perhaps as many as ten million deaths. Not surprisingly, therefore, historians have been debating the causes of this calamitous war ever since. The origins of the First World War constitute one of the most intensely studied topics in modern history - and one of the most hotly debated. Little consensus exists among historians. Perhaps this should not surprise us, since causation is such a complex issue. The causes of an event may be taken back and back into the past (just as the explanation for a traffic accident may be traced back to the inventor of the internal combustion engine, or indeed of the wheel). In this chapter we are concerned with Britain's contribution to the build-up of tension in Europe and with why Britain joined the war. This is a smaller and more manageable topic than the general issue of why the war started, but even so it poses many difficult problems. Which are the most vital areas for explaining British involvement - long-term or short-term causes, direct or indirect factors, the actions of a few powerful individuals or the unspoken assumptions of the many? Clearly, in view of this uncertainty, a wide approach must be taken.

1 The Climate of Opinion

The period from 1880 to 1914 is often described as the 'Age of Imperialism'. This is an unfortunately vague phrase, and certainly the word 'imperialism' has been used in too many contrasting ways to have any clear meaning. Some use the term to mean the acquisition of overseas colonies, some to denote the general domination - political, economic or cultural - of one country over another, and others to signify militarism, the building of bigger and more destructive armed forces. However, it has been suggested that the common factor in imperialism is an aggressive mental attitude. The imperialist believed that his country was superior to other countries, which he dismissed as inferior and treated accordingly. Such an attitude may have been one of the prime causes of the First World War.

a) Social Darwinism

One component of the imperialist world-view was Social Darwinism. This derived from the works of Charles Darwin, whose theory of evolution aroused remarkable interest, and sparked off bitter controversy, in the second half of the nineteenth century. Darwin believed that Man had not been created; instead, he had evolved from other organisms. His ideas were tentative and put forward with hesitation. But many of his followers were far more self-confident, and they believed that Darwin's thinking was important on a social, as well as a biological, level. In particular Herbert Spencer produced a highly simplified version of Darwinism, identifying its main principle as 'the survival of the fittest'. Spencer insisted that societies were like animals and that all had to struggle and fight in order to survive: those who won would grow stronger and flourish, while those who lost would decline and fall. What nations could not do was live in peace with each other. Instead, the stark options were to progress or to regress. War, therefore, was not an evil to be avoided but a means of national evolution. It was inevitable sooner or later. Nations would go to war, just as animals fought, because it was in their nature to do so. Whether war was good or bad was beside the point: morality was simply irrelevant.

b) The Image of War

In fact, the popular idea of war at the turn of the century was of a glorious adventure which would benefit its participants. This highly unrealistic view was spread by many means, including popular novels and journalism. Even Herbert Spencer found the British press too much: he gave up reading the newspapers because they 'reeked with violence'. War correspondents tended to describe battles as heroic exploits not, as they often really were, bloody massacres. One popular writer, George Steevens, insisted that war was a 'coming of age' which improved men: indeed it was 'the only quite complete holiday ever invented'! Such views were not confined to journalists. Eminent and cultured men had similar ideas. The novelist Charles Kingsley believed that war had religious sanction, in that Jesus Christ 'is not only the prince of peace: he is the prince of war too', while the art critic John Ruskin judged that 'no great art ever yet arose on earth, but among a nation of soldiers'. These notions were especially influential because they affected the education system. Many schools saw it as their job to toughen boys, preparing them to defend their country. School games had this function. Winston Churchill wrote that war seemed to him merely an extension of the violent sports he had experienced at Harrow. Out of school, boys might join the Boys' Brigade or the Boy Scouts, whose founder Baden-Powell hoped to transform youths into 'healthy patriots'. Nor were girls neglected, with the Girls' Patriotic League.

c) The Image of Foreigners

At the start of the twentieth century there was a confident belief that European nations were superior to those of other continents. Almost all

Europeans believed - with an arrogance which appears almost breathtaking to later generations - that white nations were superior to non-white. The darker the skin, it was thought, the lower was that racial group in a hierarchy of races; and only palefaces were really civilized. Racism was not only respectable around 1900, it was deemed to be a verifiable science. As a result, almost all Europeans thought incorrigibly in racial terms. But among the white nations there was thought to be a hierarchy too. Each European nation tended to look pityingly on the citizens of other states for their misfortune in being foreign. And pity often turned to contempt, if not hatred.

Certainly there was often an arrogant assumption of superiority among Britons. Some believed that the acquisition of the enormous British Empire (comprising 10 million square miles by this time) was a sign of supremacy: it testified to superior qualities of mind and body that so large a proportion of the earth's surface flew the Union Jack. Might it not even be a sign of divine approval? Perhaps God had chosen the British to civilize the rest of the world, in which case they were a new 'chosen race'. Other Europeans had fared less well in the imperial race and so tended to be dismissed as inferior. The media were full of disparaging views of foreigners, who were presented as national stereotypes not as real - and therefore varied - human beings. They were thus dehumanized. The assumption behind such presentations was that one Briton was worth any number of other nationals.

The most popular paper at the start of the century was the *Daily Mail,* with twice the circulation of its nearest rival. Its owner, Lord Northcliffe, had a low opinion of the British people, telling his journalists not to forget 'that you are writing for the meanest intelligence', and he was determined to give the public what it wanted - which, in his opinion, was 'a good hate'. He provided targets in plenty. His most successful journalist was George Steevens, whose writings presented the races and nations of the world to his readers. The Chinaman was 'deceitful above all things, and desperately wicked'; the Arab was lazy: 'give him half-an-hour and he will take an hour'; and the African was 'satisfied with his proper position of inferiority'. But Europeans were also criticised, though the French and Germans had contrasting faults:

> Frenchmen do not want to rule - they want to live. The pursuit of
> life, of laughter, of charming sensations, of intelligent apprehen-
> 5 sions, of individual development of character - it may all be more
> important, more vital to human existence than the preoccupation
> in oneself and others, to make laws and to fight. Only this you can
> say from history and from common sense: that if one nation thus
> abandons the political life while other nations still pursue it, the
> 10 solitary nation, sooner or later, will suffer from the pressure of the
> others ...

Under the Iron Heel ... It needs no customs-house to tell you that you have come into Germany. You are in a new atmosphere - an atmosphere of order, of discipline, of system, rigidly applied to the smallest detail ... You are not a person so much as the object of a direction ... The average German concentrates himself so
15 thoroughly on doing what he is told, that you are bound to wonder how much he could do if he were not told.

Clearly there was more to fear from the German than from the Frenchman, but neither had the qualities to be found in the English, who could act in a disciplined fashion without losing their individuality or initiative. Such writing was extremely popular. One observer judged that the 'British citizen breakfasts, dines, and sups on boasting and self-praise'.

d) Conclusion

Clearly a warlike climate of opinion was developing in Britain around 1900: war was presented as glorious and as inevitable, and moreover one's enemies were seen as inferior, thus making victory seem assured. The harsh realities of the Boer War did not change things much: on the contrary, the message was that Britain was vulnerable and that therefore militarisation had to be increased. However, this is not to say that only Britain was affected by such ideas. On the contrary, Social Darwinist beliefs affected most of Europe, and so did the glorious image of war and a hostile attitude to foreigners.

What real significance should be assigned to this climate of opinion? It is possible to say, with Norman Stone, that, before the declarations of war in the summer of 1914, war had already broken out 'in people's minds'. Perhaps, therefore, this is the key area for an understanding of the Great War. The diplomatic 'formalities' may be merely a consequence of this vital psychological reality: they may have provided merely the 'occasion' of war, while the fundamental 'cause' lay in the European psyche which had been conditioned to fight. Yet we should be wary of 'blanket' generalisations. First, it should be recognised that, although warlike beliefs and assumptions did exist, it is very difficult to measure their strength, especially since a peace movement existed at the same time. By concentrating on bellicose sentiments, we may fail to see them in the perspective of society as a whole. This is an area on which much more research is needed. It must also be stressed that wars start at particular times and for precise reasons. To say that the climate of opinion caused the war actually *explains* very little. We have to try to trace the consequences of the ideas and images of this period upon the politicians who made the key decisions which actually unleashed war. Hence we must turn to the more traditional concerns of the political and diplomatic historian.

2 Anglo-German Antagonism

In the last third of the nineteenth century Britain's most likely enemies had been Russia and France. In consequence, relations with Germany were relatively good. Admittedly there had been some disquiet at the military might of Prussia, especially with the wars which led to German unification in 1871, when Disraeli had asked where 'the minotaur in Berlin' would strike next; but Germany under Bismarck had proved a bulwark of the status quo. Many pointed to racial similarities between the British and the Germans, and some believed that no two nations had more in common with each other. In 1894 William Le Queux's best-selling futuristic novel, *The Great War in England in 1897,* depicted a Franco-Russian invasion of England, which was repulsed with the aid of Germany; and in 1899 the *Daily Mail* predicted that Britain and Germany might well 'have to stand shoulder to shoulder against that half-barbarian Power [Russia] that now threatens Europe'. An alliance between Germany and Britain was a distinct possibility between 1898 and 1901 (see page 82). Yet antagonism, feeding on rivalries, soon became apparent.

a) Economic Rivalry

Economic rivalry between Britain and Germany was one source of friction. *Made in Germany,* published in 1896, highlighted the extent to which German goods were penetrating the British market: it made alarming reading. The German economy had begun to grow rapidly after unification, and its production - stemming from a larger population and richer raw materials - began to rival Britain's in volume. In fact, Germany's industrial growth rate was twice as high as Britain's in the period after 1885. Already, by 1900, Germany was producing more iron and steel, and if trends continued, Germany would soon become the strongest industrial nation in Europe, and second in the world only to the United States. To Britons, who had become accustomed to economic preeminence, such developments were hard to believe yet alone accept. Furthermore, Britain began regularly to import goods of greater value than those she was exporting, producing a balance of trade deficit. Could it be that Britain was, in Social Darwinist terms, failing to win the struggle for survival?

Baden-Powell wrote in 1908 that 'Germany wants to develop her trade and commerce and must therefore get rid of England'. Such views were wildly exaggerated. Economic rivalry certainly did not make war inevitable, and indeed the British and German economies were becoming increasingly interdependent: Germany was a vastly important market for British goods, and *vice versa*. Indeed Britain was Germany's largest customer, and Germany was one of Britain's largest. No wonder capitalists in both countries thought that a war would be economic madness. Yet economic competition did help to produce an atmosphere of general rivalry and to sour international relations between the two countries.

b) The Naval Race, 1897-1914

A key factor in Anglo-German rivalry was the naval race. Britain had for centuries prided itself on the supremacy of the Royal Navy, and it was as recently as 1889 that the 'Two-Power Standard' had been adopted: Britain's navy should be as large as the next two biggest combined. This had been adopted out of fear of France and Russia, but soon Germany appeared to pose a maritime threat. Bismarck, Chancellor until 1890, had made no attempt to rival the Royal Navy, realising British sensitivity on this issue, but in 1897 Kaiser Wilhelm II adopted a policy of *Weltpolitik* (literally 'world politics'): he sought to increase the size of the German empire (calling for a 'place in the sun') and became involved in affairs outside Europe, claiming compensation when other Powers made territorial gains. Above all, he was determined to increase the size of the German navy, then only the seventh largest in the world. To further these aims, he appointed Admiral von Tirpitz as Secretary of State for the Navy, and in 1898 and 1900 legislation was passed to put in hand an important naval building programme. Three new battleships were to be built every year, while old vessels were automatically to be replaced every 25 years.

The Franco-Russian fleets were still regarded as the major threat to Britain, until the Russian defeat at Japanese hands in 1904-5, but immediately the British government became suspicious of the Germans. Why were they increasing the size of their navy? What reason could they have, if not to challenge Britain? In February 1904 the First Lord of the Admiralty insisted that the German fleet was being enlarged and modernised 'from the point of view of a war with us'. In fact, the motivation of the German leaders is not easy to fathom. At one moment it seemed that they did indeed wish to supplant Britain as the world's premier naval power, and even engage in a naval war, while at others it seemed that they merely wished to deter possible aggression from Britain or even, perhaps, to gain her respect. Or did the real reasons stem from domestic politics? The German government may well have hoped that the building of a great navy - together with a generally expansionist policy - would evoke the sort of patriotism that would transform the Kaiser into a popular hero and thereby stem the growth of opposition parties, and especially the revolutionary Social Democratic Party. But whatever the reasons, the British were aggrieved. In the press there were calls for a coup against the growing German fleet, before it was too late; and in the cabinet also worried voices were raised. Ministers insisted that while naval power might be desirable to the Germans, it was absolutely essential to Britain as a means of protecting the widely scattered Empire and commercial shipping lanes. It was also pointed out that if the German navy ever became stronger than the British, the German army would be able successfully to invade, while the small British army posed no threat to anyone. However, the Germans saw no reason to play according to rules which the British had devised.

Tirpitz aimed to construct a navy two-thirds the size of Britain's, but the British were hardly likely to sit back and watch him do so. Indeed in 1906 Britain launched HMS *Dreadnought*, an entirely new order of battleship: with ten 12-inch guns it had greater firepower than any other vessel - indeed it was more powerful than any three others combined - and with a top speed of 21 knots it could outpace anything else afloat. It seemed that the British now had a decisive lead in the naval race; but in fact this was not the case. Dreadnoughts so outclassed other battleships

PAX GERMANICA; OR, THE TEUTON DOVECOTE.

German Eagle (*to Arbitration Bird*). "NO FOREIGN DOVES REQUIRED; WE HATCH OUR OWN, THANKYOU."

Pax Germanica, Punch, *12 April 1911*

that, in a sense, all other vessels were obsolete, including Britain's, and so her existing lead was unimportant. Germany responded with its own version of the new super-ship and began widening the Kiel Canal, at enormous expense, to accommodate the larger vessels. The naval race had now reached its second, more menacing - and expensive - phase. The British cabinet was divided between the 'navalists' (wanting to outbuild Germany) and the 'economists' (who wished to cut the escalating defence budget and reach some sort of accommodation with Germany). But it was the former who won out, especially since public opinion backed them up. In 1909 'We want eight [battleships], and we won't wait' was the vociferous cry of a very vocal section of public opinion. The cabinet had been debating whether to build four or six new Dreadnoughts: now, as Churchill wryly put it, they 'finally comprom-

A LITTLE-NAVY EXHIBIT.

DESIGN FOR A FIGURE OF BRITANNIA, AS CERTAIN PEOPLE WOULD LIKE TO SEE HER.

[See reports of debate on the proposal to reduce expenditure on the Navy.]

A Little-Navy Exhibit, Punch, *22 March 1911*

ised on eight'. In view of this resolution, Britons would not have 'to turn the face of every portrait of Nelson to the wall', as one newspaper had feared might be necessary. While Germany seemed to be bristling with arms, those who recommended defence cuts in Britain were heavily criticised in the press (see the cartoons on pages 99 and 100). Within a few years Britain was spending more on her navy than Germany, France and Russia combined. Small wonder, then, that she won the naval race. The Two-Power Standard was abandoned in 1909, since the combined navies of the United States and Germany were larger than Britain's, but comfort lay in the fact that these two countries were unlikely ever to combine. British security was ensured by a 60 per cent margin of superiority over the German navy, and by a new concentration of the Royal Navy's ships in home waters. By 1912, two years before the completion of the Kiel Canal, the race was virtually over, and henceforth Germany concentrated instead on increasing the size of its army in Europe, where it seemed of little menace to Britain. The naval race was thus substantially over several years before the First World War began. Naval rivalry, therefore, was not a direct cause of the war. Yet nor is it irrelevant to it, for nothing so harmed Anglo-German relations, convinced British politicians that Germany was a potential enemy, or prepared each nation psychologically for war against the other. In Britain it produced an intense 'Germanophobia'. Invasion scares were now centred on Germany, not Russia or France. The classic exposition of this was *The Riddle of the Sands,* a best-selling novel published in 1903. Le Queux jumped on the bandwagon, producing his even more successful *The Invasion of 1910.* It was around this time that people scoured the countryside looking for German spies disguised (in what was supposed to be typical Teutonic guise) as barbers or waiters. Furthermore, anti-German feeling was shown by the large membership of the Navy League, campaigning for a larger navy, and the National Service League, which wished to see the introduction of conscription.

c) The First Moroccan Crisis, 1905

Before the naval race had reached its second phase, an international crisis rocked Anglo-German relations. Britain had recently signed the *Entente Cordiale* with France, by which the French accepted British rule in Egypt in return for recognition of their interests in Morocco (see page 88). This was not an anti-German move, and yet the Germans seemed to feel menaced by it. Already the Franco-Russian alliance of 1894 appeared dangerous to Berlin; now a French understanding with Britain, and its powerful navy, would further undermine German security by threatening encirclement (with Russia to the east, France to the west, and the Royal Navy to the north, in the North Sea). The Kaiser's government therefore tried to break the Entente before it had had time fully to gel. This is the probable motive for Wilhelm II's provocative action of landing at Tangier in March 1905 as the champion of Morocco's independence. Anticipating that the international community would resist French control, he refused talks with France and insisted instead that an international conference be called to decide Morocco's future. Almost certainly he believed that Britain would fail to support France if it began to seem that a war might ensue, and in this way a wedge would be driven between the Entente Powers. Yet it is impossible to be certain of German motives, and some historians believe that the Kaiser actually wanted a war: certainly the temporary weakness of Russia, after its defeat by Japan, made this an opportune time for German aggression against France.

German motives were no clearer to the French and British governments. Foreign Secretary Lansdowne called the German 'escapade' an 'extraordinarily clumsy bit of diplomacy'. The advocate of a German alliance a few years earlier, he now regretfully acknowledged that such a goal was no longer realistic. Yet he disliked the anti-German tone of the British press, and he refused to guarantee that, if a war did start, Britain would support France against Germany. His successor at the end of 1905, the Liberal Sir Edward Grey, also refused to issue such a guarantee, but in fact Grey had fewer qualms: while not speaking for the whole government, much less for future administrations, he told the French ambassador that, in his personal opinion, Britain would support France if she were attacked by Germany. Certainly he was solidly behind France - and orchestrated support from Russia, Spain, and Italy - when an international conference met at Algeçiras early in 1906 to settle the Moroccan issue. The result was that Germany was isolated and outvoted, while France's interests were substantially endorsed. Furthermore, Britain and France emerged from the crisis as much closer collaborators than before. The *Entente Cordiale* had thus been strengthened not weakened, and it had also assumed an anti-German character. Heavy-handed German diplomacy had, paradoxically, conjured up what it had sought to destroy. At the same time, by exacerbating tensions in western Europe, it was creating a long-term cause of the First World War.

d) Sir Edward Grey

At the height of the first Moroccan crisis Grey had authorised military talks with the French, without consulting the cabinet, and had even considered despatching an expeditionary force to the continent. Such unparalleled planning signalled a severe deterioration in Anglo-German relations, especially when coupled with the building of the Dreadnoughts from this same year (1906). Grey obviously looked upon Germany as the real threat to peace in Europe.

Many contemporaries, and subsequent historians, have praised the work of Grey as Foreign Secretary (from December 1905 to December

1916). To his 'supporters', this landowning gentleman, educated at Winchester and Balliol College, Oxford, was not only extremely competent but also highly principled and honourable, someone who was above the ruck of normal party politics and therefore able to appeal to Conservatives as well as Liberals. He was thus more statesman than politician. He has been praised for settling disputes with Russia in 1907, an agreement which brought about the Triple Entente (see page 88); and although he failed to bring about good relations with Germany, it has been argued that this was not through any fault of his but because of German aggressive tendencies. When war was unavoidable, in 1914, he entered the conflict, with patent reluctance, because there was no other choice. However, others considered him little short of a disaster as Foreign Secretary.

Grey's 'opponents' point out that he was an insular figure. He spoke no foreign language, had never been abroad until May 1914, and was ignorant of European geography, especially the Balkan region. He also insisted on going fishing or bird-watching at weekends, no matter how many international storm clouds were brewing. Indeed he has been portrayed as obsessed with eliminating Anglo-Russian tension and as being unreasonably anti-German. He is said to have given unwarranted attention to the views of the Foreign Office officials, who arrogantly considered that they always knew best. He was also highly secretive, rarely revealing his mind fully and not always taking important issues to the cabinet. It is not that he was more secretive than, say, Lord Salisbury had been, but that public and political expectations had changed since the end of the nineteenth century and so he should have been more open, especially since he was the first foreign secretary since 1865 to sit in the House of Commons rather than the Lords. Lloyd George was to complain of the 'ridiculously small percentage of time devoted to foreign affairs' by the cabinet. Perhaps Grey realised that the Liberal cabinet, containing its fair share of isolationist 'Little Englanders' as well as expansionist 'Imperialists', might reject his policies. It is hard to be certain on this point. All we can say conclusively is that Grey, an aloof and reticent man by temperament, was an elusive figure. Small wonder that a third group, of contemporaries and historians, has regarded him as an enigma.

There can be no doubt that several influential officials at the Foreign Office, and in particular the senior clerk Eyre Crowe, were highly suspicious of German intentions. In January 1907 Crowe wrote a wide-ranging and important memorandum. He insisted that while he was uncertain that Germany was aiming at the hegemony of Europe - its foreign policy being perhaps too erratic to support such a clear-cut interpretation - Britain had every reason to be wary.

1 If it be considered necessary to formulate and accept a theory that will fit all the ascertained facts of German foreign policy, the choice

must lie between the two hypotheses here presented: Either
Germany is definitely aiming at a general political ascendancy,
5 threatening the independence of her neighbours and ultimately the
existence of England;
   Or Germany, free from any such clear-cut ambition, and
thinking for the present merely of using her legitimate position and
influence as one of the leading Powers in the council of nations, is
10 seeking to promote her foreign commerce, spread the benefits of
German culture, extend the scope of her national energies, and
create fresh German interests all over the world ...
   The choice offered is a narrow one, nor easy to make with any
close approach to certainty. It will, however, be seen on reflection,
15 that there is no actual necessity for a British government to
determine definitely which of the two theories of German policy it
will accept. For it is clear that the second scheme (of
semi-independent evolution, not entirely unaided by statecraft)
may at any stage merge into the first, or conscious-design scheme.
20 Moreover, if ever the evolution scheme should come to be realised,
the position thereby accruing to Germany would obviously
constitute as formidable a menace to the rest of the world as would
be presented by any deliberate conquest of a similar position by
'malice aforethought' ...
25   So long as England remains faithful to the general principle of
the preservation of the balance of power, her interests would not be
served by Germany being reduced to the rank of a weak Power, as
this might easily lead to a Franco-Russian predominance equally, if
not more, formidable to the British Empire ...
30   Germany will think twice before she now gives rise to any fresh
disagreements ... if she meets on England's part with unvarying
courtesy and consideration in all matters of common concern, but
also with a prompt and firm refusal to enter into any one-sided
bargains or arrangements, and the most unbending determination
35 to uphold British rights and interests in every part of the globe.
There will be no surer or quicker way to win the respect of the
German Government and of the German nation.

Crowe believed that Britain would have to oppose German ambitions
resolutely and firmly. How far Grey was influenced by these views, and
how far he already shared them, is uncertain. What is certain, however,
is that in 1911 he had occasion to apply this strategy.

e) The Second Moroccan Crisis (Agadir), 1911

At the beginning of July 1911 a second storm blew up over Morocco.
French troops had recently occupied Fez, the capital city, after a
rebellion led the Sultan to call for their help. It looked likely that France

would soon establish a protectorate over the whole country, thus breaking the terms of the Algeçiras conference, and at this point Germany intervened. A German gunboat, the *Panther*, arrived at the port of Agadir. Why had the Germans intervened? The Foreign Office decided that the aim was, as in 1905, to destroy the Entente; but it is much more likely that the Germans simply wanted to secure a foreign policy success. They promised to recognise French control of Morocco providing the French would cede territory in Africa. In this way, German strategists believed, Franco-German relations would improve, while territorial concessions would bring popularity at home in Germany. Yet things did not go according to plan. The French were aggrieved that the Germans were demanding so much territory, in fact the whole of the French Congo, so that Franco-German relations deteriorated, and Britain decided that it had so show firmness if German ambitions were to be kept within bounds.

Asquith's Liberal cabinet was divided on how to treat Germany. A pro-German faction wished to see improved relations, especially because the expensive naval race was hampering the implementation of schemes of social reform. Hence when Grey argued that Britain, like Germany, should send a vessel to Morocco he was overruled. But, even so, this crisis convinced several 'doves', and in particular the Chancellor of the Exchequer, David Lloyd George - commonly believed to be a 'Little Englander', and admittedly a man who had opposed the Boer War - that German ambitions had to be countered. At the Mansion House, towards the end of July, he warned that, although he would make great sacrifices to preserve peace, 'if a situation were to be forced upon us in which peace could only be preserved ... by allowing Britain to be treated where her interests were vitally affected as if she were of no account in the Cabinet of nations, then I say emphatically that peace at that price would be a humiliation intolerable for a great country like ours to endure'. Yet the speech probably did more harm than good. A majority in Britain greeted it with enthusiasm, but it produced universal indignation in Germany.

A Franco-German crisis was rapidly becoming an Anglo-German one. Indeed war seemed possible, so that once more Grey endorsed military talks with the French, this time more detailed than in 1905-6. Plans were worked out for the despatch of an expeditionary force to the continent, and the British fleet was put on the alert. Nevertheless, in the end Germany accepted limited territorial concessions in Africa, and France duly established its protectorate over Morocco the following year. The crisis was over, but only at the cost of greatly increasing tensions between the Great Powers, and in particular between Britain and Germany.

The Agadir crisis undoubtedly led to more belligerent attitudes in Europe. More and more people began to accept the Social Darwinist idea that a major war was inevitable sooner or later. Germany soon decided to increase the size of its army, the Russians began an even more dramatic expansion programme, and the French extended their period of conscription from two to three years. As for Britain, besides new military talks with the French, the combative Winston Churchill was appointed First Lord of the Admiralty. Asquith's government had not formally committed itself, but many believed that, if it came to war, France would receive support from Britain. In retrospect, we can see that the outbreak of the First World War had come appreciably nearer.

3 British Foreign Policy, 1912-14

Yet despite the dangers of war around 1911, Asquith's Liberal government did not accept that war with Germany was inevitable. Indeed in 1912 Lord Haldane, the Secretary of State for War, was sent to Berlin to try to achieve better relations. His mission was boosted by renewed tensions with Russia over Persia. The Russians seemed to be breaking their 1907 Entente with Britain, and there were fears for the security of British India. Certainly the Viceroy said he could put very little faith in Russian pledges, and a senior official at the India Office accused the Russians of 'bad faith'. Unless better relations with Germany could be secured, therefore, Britain might become dangerously dependent upon its Entente partner.

Haldane held talks with the Kaiser and Tirpitz, and also with the Chancellor, Bethmann-Hollweg, a man who had put out feelers for an Anglo-German *rapprochement* and who was reckoned - quite rightly - to be far more conciliatory than the other two. But no agreement was reached. The Germans wanted British neutrality in the event of a Franco-German or Russo-German war, and, in return, they offered to scale down their naval construction programme. But all Haldane promised was that Britain would not pursue an aggressive policy towards Germany. He would not accept an unqualified neutrality that would compromise Britain's freedom of action and, in effect, amount to her abdication from European affairs. The request also seemed sinister. What aggressive moves might Germany be hatching? Haldane's view was endorsed by a majority of the Liberal cabinet, though a minority, harking back to the traditions of Cobden and Bright (see page 3), believed that standing aside from continental squabbles was the best policy to pursue.

Far fewer Anglo-French mutual suspicions existed, and so it was much easier to do a deal with France. The French government would have liked a full-scale alliance, including a commitment that Britain would defend France against a German attack. But Grey would not go this far, perhaps fearing that a guarantee of support might encourage the French to be too adventurous. He did, however, sign a naval agreement with France in 1913: the French would guard the Mediterranean, thus freeing British vessels for other duties; and, in return, the Royal Navy would patrol the English Channel. The upshot of the agreement was that Britain undertook, though informally, responsibility for the defence of parts of the French coastline. In conjunction with the military talks of 1911, this agreement amounted almost to a synchronisation of Anglo-French defence policies; and it made it very likely - though not absolutely certain - that, in any war involving France and Germany, Britain would not be neutral: instead she would fight alongside her neighbouring Entente partner. British foreign policy was clearer than for decades past. But alongside clarity went immense dangers. Grey's critics believed that the Entente was being transformed into an alliance. The sort of commitment which Lord Salisbury had always managed to avoid had been all but undertaken by Sir Edward Grey.

a) Improved Anglo-German Relations

Yet, against the odds, the international climate soon improved for Britain. There were problems aplenty in European affairs, but these were in eastern Europe. Already, in 1908, a crisis had erupted over Bosnia and Herzegovina, two provinces of the Ottoman Empire which the Austrians had controlled since the Congress of Berlin of 1878. When it seemed that the Turks might reassert their control, Austria stepped in and annexed the territory, to the dismay of Russia and Serbia, its client state (see the map on page 28). Any breach of the status quo in the Balkans raised the fears of Austria and Russia, two Great Powers with important interests in this area - Austria because the growth of Slav nationalism might lead its own Slavs to attempt to quit the multi-national Austrian Empire, Russia because it was the traditional defender of the Slavs and because it needed passage through the Dardanelles if it was to be considered a truly European Power (see page 4). This situation led to two wars, in 1912 and 1913, in the Balkans.

In the first Balkan war, in 1911, a League led by Serbia waged war on Turkey. The Austrian generals, fearing the expansion of Serbia, were in favour of joining the war on the Turkish side, despite the fact that Russia might then enter, but the Austrian Prime Minister calmed the situation down, partly in the hope that Turkey would win the war unaided. However, the Balkan League defeated Turkey, and the war was ended when Sir Edward Grey successfully urged the Powers to accept a conference of ambassadors, under his chairmanship, in London. He found the Germans particularly co-operative, and the war was settled by the Treaty of London of May 1913. However, the former allies, Serbia and Bulgaria, soon began the second Balkan war: they were quarrelling over the spoils of victory. This time the Austrian civilians, as well as the military, were in favour of fighting against Serbia, but the Germans refused to agree to intervention: after all, the Balkan rivals might fight to mutual exhaustion, destroying each other in the process. But again this reasoning was not borne out by events. Serbia won the war, gaining land in the process under the terms of the harsh Treaty of Bucharest. In fact, Serbia had almost doubled in size over the previous few years, and so the Austrians were determined - and sooner rather than later - to destroy their hated rivals. The fact that, in 1911 and 1912, the Great Powers had stayed out of the conflict because of miscalculation - in other words, luck - made it seem extremely unlikely that major war could be long postponed. Austria and Serbia would surely go to war, and Austria would call for German support, while Serbia would look to Russia. It is with justification that the Balkans have been called the 'tinder box' of Europe. One more spark might ignite a major conflagration.

However, now that international attention was centred on eastern Europe rather than Morocco, it seemed possible that Britain - and even France - might not be involved. Britain was an anxious spectator of the Balkan crises rather than an active participant, its role being limited to one of impartial mediation, as Grey strove to resurrect Gladstone's ideal of the Concert of Europe. Britain's own safety seemed reasonably secure: it rested on good relations with the United States, on the alliance with Japan, on naval supremacy, and on the Ententes. Furthermore, by the summer of 1914 Anglo-German relations were better than for a long time. The naval race was over, despite the opening of the Kiel Canal, and the two rivals had agreed on the building of the Baghdad railway in Mesopotamia, as well as settling quite amicably their disagreements over the future of Portugal's colonies. 'Since I have been at the Foreign Office,' wrote one official, 'I have not seen such calm waters'. Grey was of the same mind, insisting that the 'German government are in a peaceful mood and ... are very anxious to be on good terms with England'. In June 1914 five eminent Germans received honorary degrees at Oxford, and in July Lloyd George insisted that 'the sky has never been more perfectly blue'. He called for defence cuts in the next budget because relations with Germany had never been better. Admittedly on 28 June the heir to the Austrian throne, Franz Ferdinand, had been shot in Bosnia's capital, Sarajevo, but this seemed to herald merely a renewal of the Balkan problems and, at worst, a third Balkan war. The assassination was overshadowed in the British press by the death of Joseph Chamberlain a few days later. Yet within a few weeks Britain had entered the most destructive war in its history.

4 The Outbreak of War

The assassination began a chain-reaction of events. First, the Austrians decided that they now had the ideal pretext to take firm action against Serbia. That Serbian complicity in the death of the Emperor's nephew had not been proven did not matter: Serbia's crime was simply to exist. Next the Austrians had to secure support from their German ally, since Serbia was likely to be backed up by Russia. On 5 July the Kaiser gave a 'blank cheque': he promised unconditional support. The Austrians then delivered an ultimatum to Serbia on 23 July. This was over three weeks after the assassination, but it took some time to devise conditions so difficult that Serbs would inevitably be unable to accept them. Delivery was also delayed because the French president was visiting Russia and it was thought unwise to present the ultimatum - described by Grey as the 'most formidable document I have ever seen addressed by one state to another that was independent' - when the Franco-Russian allies were together. Two days later Serbia issued a conciliatory reply, but one which did not accept all Austrian demands. Austria therefore declared war on Serbia (28 July), the Russians then decided to mobilise their forces, and on 1 August Germany declared war on Russia. In a few tense, dramatic and - it must be admitted - highly confused days, the condition of Europe had been transformed. War was about to start. But would Britain participate?

a) Britain's Decision

The British cabinet was hard at work in June and July 1914 considering the problems posed in Ireland by the Home Rule movement. Many Liberals wished to concede Home Rule to the Catholic majority, but this conflicted with the determination of the Protestants of Ulster to maintain the union with Britain. Moreover, the Ulstermen were supported by the British Conservative party. A violent clash - in fact, civil war in Ireland - seemed a distinct possibility. In view of these pressing problems, the international situation seemed relatively unimportant. There might well be another war in far-off eastern Europe, but surely Britain would not be involved. Grey was definitely optimistic. In fact he had been told by the German ambassador that the Kaiser would restrain his Austrian ally from strong action against Serbia following the assassination. It was not until 24 July, when he received details of the ultimatum, that Grey realised he had been misled. At this stage the cabinet discussed European affairs for the first time that summer. But still there was no sense of urgency. Grey broached the idea of renewing the ambassadors' conference in London but soon decided to take a fishing holiday in Hampshire. Asquith confided to his mistress the gloomy news that 'We are in measurable distance of Armageddon', but he added, more cheerfully: 'Happily there seems ... no reason why we should be more than spectators'. Many Liberals decided that a war in eastern Europe was essentially none of their business. Grey said that if the war were confined to the east he would 'take a holiday tomorrow'. If the French became involved, that would change the situation; but, even so, several cabinet ministers judged that Germany/Austria and Russia/France were evenly matched. Britain would still be able to stand aside, especially since the small British army, though improved in quality over recent years, would make no appreciable difference either way.

However, there were those in the Foreign Office, especially Eyre Crowe, who had different views. He had long wanted to transform the Entente with France into an alliance, and he judged that if France entered the war Britain would have to do likewise. Germany was aiming at 'the political dictatorship of Europe', a fact which Britain could not ignore, especially since its military conversations with France created a 'moral bond' and an 'honourable expectation of British support'. Indeed the French ambassador, anxious to learn how Britain would react, told Grey that he was 'waiting to know if the word honour should be erased from the English language'. The Foreign Secretary - who, it has been said, had the code of morality of a nineteenth-century public schoolboy - could not but take this moral challenge seriously. The Russians also applied pressure, urging Grey to declare that, if it came to war in Europe, Britain would fight with her Entente partners: unless he did so, war would be rendered *more* likely. This was sound reasoning, from one point of view; but, on the other hand, perhaps Britain might be a more effective mediator if clearly neutral.

How, then, would the government react? On 27 July, when Grey first broached the possibility of Britain entering a war if Germany attacked France, five members of the cabinet warned that they would resign. Two days later, one minister summed up another meeting with the words, 'It was decided not to decide'. The Foreign Secretary's offers of mediation had been turned down flat by Germany, and he was becoming convinced that the German militarists were deliberately inflaming the crisis. He therefore believed that Britain could have to fight, and he was supported forcefully by Churchill and Haldane, but without cabinet agreement he was powerless. He therefore told the French ambassador 'Don't count on our coming in', while to the German ambassador he warned 'Don't count on our staying out'.

Much obviously depended on whether the French would join the war. Germany declared war on Russia on 1 August, but would the French support their ally? As a precautionary measure, on 2 August, the British cabinet warned Germany against attacking the French coast. The Germans were extremely unlikely to take such an action, and, if they did, British involvement in a naval war was more acceptable to the cabinet than the despatch of an army to the continent. But, even so, one member of the cabinet resigned, and the majority still hoped to stay out. Indeed Asquith wrote in his diary on 2 August, 'I suppose a good three-quarters of our own party in the House of Commons are for absolute non-interference at any price'. The omens for British neutrality were boosted when the German ambassador gave an assurance that, if the French stayed neutral in a Russo-German war, Germany would not attack them.

Yet once again this ambassador had given false information. On the following day (3 August) Germany declared war on France. The Germans were committed to the Schlieffen Plan: in order to avoid a war on two fronts, the Germans intended first to knock out France, within a matter of weeks, and then move their forces eastwards to face the larger, but more slowly mobilising, Russian army. Finally the British government had to clarify its position. Would they intervene or not? The issue was still highly uncertain. The *Entente Cordiale* did not necessitate British support for France, and neither did the military or naval talks held after the Moroccan crises. It is true that Britain, and several other Powers, had guaranteed Belgian neutrality by the Treaty of London of 1839 and that, in their invasion of France, German troops were bound to violate that neutrality. But would such a violation necessitate British intervention? The cabinet had already decided that, legally, there would be no obligation for Britain alone to intervene. Asquith told the king that support for Belgium, if it arose, would be 'rather one of policy than of legal obligation'. If the other guarantors (including Germany!) failed to act, Britain would not have to. Indeed Britain might actually be breaking international law by intervening unless the Belgians called for assistance, and it seemed very unlikely they would do so, providing the Germans, as anticipated, marched through the Ardennes, in southern Belgium. Access to France along this route would not involve any occupation of Belgian soil and so would cause minimum inconvenience and provoke minimum Belgian response. Providing the Germans took this route, therefore, Britain would be unable to intervene, and the cabinet would have to face the momentous issue of whether to support France.

An important factor was added to the equation at this stage. The Conservatives made it known that they were very much in favour of intervention: the Opposition leaders informed the cabinet that 'it would be fatal to the honour and security of the United Kingdom to hesitate in supporting France and Russia'. Thus it seemed quite possible that, if the Liberal government could not agree on a policy, it would be replaced by a Conservative administration, or a coalition, which would enter the war.

Asquith and his cabinet were in a desperately difficult position, and Grey was on the verge of resignation. Relief came on 3 August when they learned that the Germans were demanding passage through the whole of Belgium, thus unexpectedly sparking a Belgian call for assistance. Many members of the cabinet, like Lloyd George, who had formerly been unable to make up their minds, now came down firmly in favour of war. In addition, there were unmistakable signs that public opinion favoured intervention. Demonstrations were taking place in Trafalgar Square, and crowds - deluded by the belief that a war would be all over by Christmas - assembled outside Buckingham Palace shouting 'We want war!' A police guard had to be mounted to protect the German Embassy. Powerful pro-war and anti-German feelings, which had been smouldering for many years, now surfaced, removing the last vestiges of doubt from the Liberal cabinet. Only the veteran John Morley resigned. The invasion of Belgium seemed a clear-cut case of naked aggression against a weaker neighbour, as in *Punch's* cartoon (see below). Grey's speech to the House of Commons convinced MPs that Britain should issue an ultimatum, preparatory to war with Germany - not that they needed much convincing.

1 How far [Anglo-French] friendship entails obligations ... let every
  man look into his own heart, and his own feelings, and construe the
  extent of the obligation for himself. I construe it myself as I feel it ...
  If her [Belgium's] independence goes, the independence of
5 Holland will follow. I ask the House from the point of view of
  British interests, to consider what may be at stake. If France is
  beaten in a struggle of life and death, beaten to her knees, loses her
  position as a Great Power, becomes subordinate to the will of one

Bravo, Belgium!, Punch, *19 August 1914*

greater than herself ...? It may be said, I suppose, that we might
10 stand aside, husband our strength, and that whatever happened in
the course of the war at the end of it intervene with effect to put
things right, and to adjust them to our point of view. If, in a crisis
like this, we run away from those obligations of honour and interest
15 as regards the Belgian Treaty, I doubt whether, whatever material
force we might have at the end, it would be of very much value in
face of the respect that we should have lost. And do not believe,
whether a great Power stands outside this war or not, it is going to
be in a position at the end of it to exert its superior strength. For us,
20 with a powerful Fleet, which we believe able to protect our
commerce, to protect our shores and to protect our interests, if we
are engaged in war, we shall suffer but little more than we shall
suffer even if we stand aside.

With intervention presented in this way - as a mixture of self-interest and
honour, and moreover as not unduly onerous - parliament was in favour.
Britain declared war on Germany on 4 August.

5 Conclusion

Great Britain was an important participant in the First World War and
played a significant role in its origins. But it should be recognised that
Britain was not as important for the actual *outbreak* of the war as were
Austria, Germany, Serbia, Russia and France. After all, a major war was
already under way when Britain joined. In addition, British ministers did
not positively want war, and they entered with patent reluctance and
without any jingoistic enthusiasm. Grey, with tears in his eyes, told the
American ambassador that he felt 'like a man who has wasted his life'.
More portentously, he added that 'The lamps are going out all over
Europe; we shall not see them lit again in our lifetime'. Indeed Britain
cannot be said to have *caused* the conflict at all, except insofar as the war
came about through long and medium-term factors such as the arms
race, imperial rivalry and the development of a warlike climate of
opinion.

But why did Britain enter the war? It is sometimes said that the Great
Powers in 1914 went to war in order to solve their domestic problems.
But although this may be true of the imperial governments in Austria or
Germany, there seems little to recommend the theory in the case of
Britain. It is quite true that Ireland posed momentous problems, as did a
wave of industrial discontent and the increasingly militant suffragettes;
and it is also correct that, for a time, such problems disappeared in the
welter of patriotism that marked the start of the war. But there is no
direct evidence that Asquith's government entered the war because of
domestic difficulties. Cabinet discussions dealt exclusively with the
European situation and its ramifications for Britain in Europe. Perhaps

domestic issues may have influenced the policy-makers unconsciously to some degree, but we cannot be sure even of this.

Did Britain enter in defence of 'gallant little Belgium'? Clearly ministers did not declare war on Germany only for Belgium. After all, the government had been prepared to turn a blind eye if the Germans had moved through southern Belgium, a fact conveniently forgotten once the war had begun. The notion that Britain entered the war solely because the Germans had violated Belgian neutrality was in fact effective propaganda, endowing the British with a just and unselfish cause. The invasion of Belgium was important, since it allowed the Liberals to join the war with a relatively united front, with only two resignations, and it certainly determined the exact timing of Britain's entry. Yet most historians believe that Britain would have entered the war anyway, sooner or later, though perhaps not with a Liberal administration. This view is based upon the notion that there was a variety of good reasons for British participation.

These included Anglo-German rivalry, which is often seen as the root cause of Britain's entry. Germany was growing stronger and stronger, threatening Britain's preeminence, and it seemed that Europe was simply not big enough for two such Powers. The British had resigned themselves to the supremacy of the United States in the new world, but Germany was too geographically close for a similar accommodation. Public opinion (fed by Social Darwinist assumptions and the glorious image of war) provides another important explanation. No government could afford to neglect the demonstrations of 3 August. This is not to say that the demonstrations represented the considered opinions of all British citizens. No doubt there were many who hoped Britain would stay out of the conflict, but these people did not take to the streets. A journalist recalled that Asquith did not carry England into the war; on the contrary, England carried Asquith. 'A House of Commons that had hesitated an hour after the invasion of Belgium would have been swept out of existence by the wrath and indignation of the people'. Certainly it must have seemed like that in the heady days of early August 1914. Asquith's government did not share public enthusiasm for war but it could not afford to ignore it.

Above all, perhaps, perceptions of the national interest led to Britain's declaration of war. The outcome of war was inevitably uncertain to some degree, but what might happen if Britain stayed out? Undoubtedly British prestige would suffer, and so might more material interests. By the end of the war, both sides might have fought to mutual exhaustion, leaving Britain the dominant Power in Europe. To some, this would seem the best of all possible outcomes, but in this case British trade with an impoverished continent would necessarily suffer. This was bad enough, but what if one side won? If Germany and her allies won, then Britain would be isolated and in danger of losing a renewed period of Anglo-German antagonism. Perhaps, sooner or later, a victorious

Germany would attack Britain. If, on the other hand, Russia won, then would the situation have been any easier for the British? There would be problems in Europe, the Middle East and Asia, difficulties made all the more severe by Britain's unwillingness during the July Crisis to throw its weight behind the Triple Entente. Either way, the balance of power in Europe would be destroyed, to Britain's substantial disadvantage. This was the reasoning which led *The Times* on 6 August 1914 to endorse the government's actions. It described intervention as being 'not merely a duty of friendship. It is ... an elementary duty of self-preservation ... We cannot stand alone in a Europe dominated by any single power'.

a) Alternative Policies

There were many reasons why Britain joined the war in August 1914, but this is not to say that the policy followed by the government was the wisest one. Indeed Grey's foreign policy has over the decades been criticised in two ways. First, some say that instead of joining the Triple Entente, he should have maintained stricter neutrality in European affairs. This view was put forward by Liberal critics at the time (including Morley) and it has often been reiterated. It is an easy criticism to make, but would it have been an easy policy to pursue? There were dangers in isolation, as Salisbury well knew. Nor had Grey committed himself irrevocably to France and Russia. He had indeed kept in close contact with Germany, as shown by Haldane's mission of 1912 and the (fruitful) Anglo-German contacts of the first six months of 1914. Was Grey's policy so very different from Salisbury's wish to be associated with the European powers while avoiding entangling alliances? The Ententes were not alliances. It must be said that Grey had teetered on the brink - with Anglo-French military planning - of committing Britain in a way which Salisbury would probably have deplored. But had he fallen over the brink? When a Foreign Office official insisted that Grey had again and again 'promised' the French ambassador that Britain would stand by France if Germany attacked, the Foreign Secretary replied - with words which must surely have stuck in his honourable throat - 'Yes, but he has nothing in writing'.

On the other hand, Grey has also been criticised for *not* making the Entente into a real alliance. A pledge of British support for France might, so the argument runs, have deterred the Germans from aggressive actions during the war crisis of 1914. Lloyd George insisted in his *War Memoirs* that in 1914 Grey had been 'a pilot whose hand trembled in the palsy of apprehension, unable to grip the levers with a firm and clear purpose'. Had Grey 'warned Germany in time of the point at which Britain would declare war - and wage it with her whole strength - the issue would have been different'. Yet there are objections to this line of argument as well. First, it was not possible for Grey alone to form such an alliance, and the Liberal cabinet would probably not have countenanced such a departure from previous policy. Secondly, would the Germans really have been restrained by a united front between Britain, France and Russia? There is much doubt on this issue. Bethmann-Hollweg certainly would have been. He was distraught when he found, in August 1914, that Britain was to enter the war, especially to defend Belgium because of the old 1839 treaty - a 'scrap of paper'. But the Chancellor in 1914 did not have the political authority Bismarck had once commanded; and at a meeting of the German cabinet on 1 August, when the Germans declared war after receiving the news of Russian mobilisation, the Kaiser expressed his great satisfaction at the way events had worked out: all he needed to make his happiness complete, he insisted, was for Britain to enter the war. Bethmann's attempt to reverse German policy, on Britain's entry, was therefore overruled. The fact that Britain did not have a strong army in 1914 made its 'weight' as a potential enemy less than formidable to most key figures in Germany.

Much depends on the issue of whether the Germans in the summer of 1914 deliberately desired a war (as historians such as Fritz Fischer have argued) or whether they simply stumbled into war (as historians such as A.J.P. Taylor have insisted). Either way, it is not easy to see how Britain could have averted conflict, especially since, during the last few days of peace, the military élites in Germany and Russia were increasingly taking over from the politicians and implementing their inflexible mobilisation plans. Perhaps other policies might have served British interests better than the ones the Asquith government followed. After all, almost anything is possible! The issue will long be debated. But it is not at all easy to say with certainty what those policies should have been. Perhaps, sooner or later, Britain had to fight or abdicate as a Great Power.

Making notes on 'Britain and the Origins of the First World War'

Your notes need to be detailed on this important chapter, and you will need to integrate material from the previous chapter on the two Moroccan crises. Pay special attention to the actual outbreak of war in July and August 1914.

The headings and sub-headings should help you to organise your notes. But, as for the last chapter, you might also compile parallel notes on Britain's relations with separate countries. It would also be useful to try to construct some sort of 'model' of the causes of the war. Use the terms with which you are familiar: perhaps you might employ words such as 'preconditions' (the longer-term factors without which war could not have occurred), 'precipitants' (the main factors which actually helped to produce the war) and 'triggers' (short-term factors which determined the precise timing of events which were very likely to happen anyway, sooner or later). Can all the relevant causes of the war be

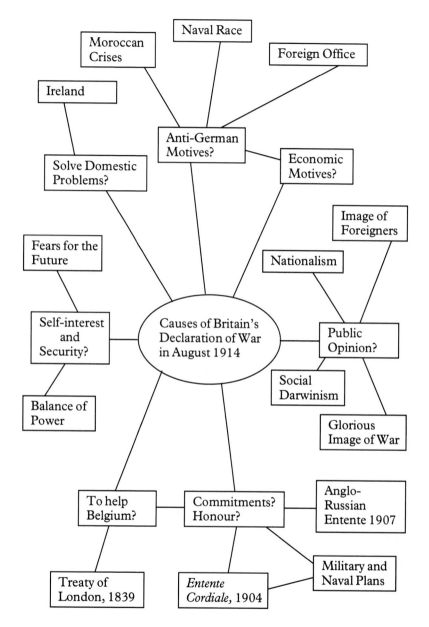

Summary - Britain and the Origins of the First World War

grouped under this tripartite division? Other useful terms are 'sufficient factor' (a cause which on its own is enough to explain an event) and 'necessary factor' (a cause which is necessary to the event, i.e. but for which the event could not have taken place). And do not neglect 'short-term' and 'long-term', and perhaps 'medium-term'. Whichever selection of terms you make, try to estimate the importance of each cause by comparing it with others, and attempt to assign it as precise a 'role' as possible in bringing about the war.

Answering essay questions on 'Britain and the Origins of the First World War'

Questions on this topic are extremely common. Consider the following titles:

1   How successful were the Liberals in dealing with defence and foreign policy issues between 1905 and 1914?
2   What were the aims of British foreign policy between 1905 and 1914 and how successfully were they implemented?
3   What determined the relationship between Britain and Germany in the period from 1882 to 1914?
4   For what reasons, and by what stages, did Britain and Germany move towards hostility in the period 1900-1914?
5   Why did Britain and France form and maintain a close friendship in the years from 1900 to 1914?
6   Discuss the view that Sir Edward Grey's foreign policy led inevitably to Britain's declaration of war on Germany in 1914.
7   'Britain had little choice but to enter the World War in August 1914.' Discuss this view.
8   To what extent did Britain enter the First World war in order to protect Belgian independence?

Look in particular at question 8, variations on which are extremely common. For instance, 'to maintain the balance of power' might be substituted for 'to protect Belgian independence'. Try tackling an essay plan for the version of the question as it stands. In effect, you are being asked to compare the importance of protecting Belgian independence as a motive for entering the war with other possible motives. Hence you must decide what these other motives were. What would you include besides the wish to maintain the balance of power, fear of German expansion, and the desire to support Entente partners? Next you must decide the relative importance of the Belgian factor. You may possibly decide that the wish to maintain Belgium's integrity was of relatively little significance, compared with other factors, but even so you must spend a sizable proportion of your answer on this issue - after all, this is the issue singled out in the title. If, therefore, you think the factor unimportant, you must marshal evidence in support of your view and argue your case, not merely assert it. 'How far' questions often involve comparing the importance of one factor, specified in the title, with other factors, often unspecified. The time you spend evaluating or weighing the relative importance of different causes of an event will provide valuable practice for this very important type of question.

Source-based questions on 'Britain and the Origins of the First World War'

1 George Steevens on France and Germany
Read the extracts on pages 95-6 and answer the following questions.
a) Put into your own words Steevens' criticisms of the French.
   (3 marks)
b) What is the significance of the sub-title 'Under the Iron Heel'?
   (3 marks)
c) Why do you think that the British had more to fear from the Germans than the French? (4 marks)
d) How historically valuable are these extracts? Explain your answer.
   (5 marks)

2 Two cartoons from *Punch*
Study the two cartoons on pages 99 and 100 and answer the following questions.
a) In the 'Little-Navy Exhibit', identify the 'certain people' who wished to see Britannia like this. (1 mark)
b) What aspects of the British Lion and of Britannia particularly exhibit their weakness? (4 marks)
c) What features of 'Pax Germanica' emphasise Germany's strength? (3 marks)
d) What is the significance of the Union Jack carried by the smaller bird? (2 marks)
e) How historically accurate do you consider the two cartoons? Explain your answer. (5 marks)

3 Eyre Crowe's memorandum, January 1907
Read the extract on pages 103-4 and answer the following questions.
a) What events to you think Crowe had in mind when he wrote of 'all the ascertained facts of German foreign policy' (line 2)? Do you think that these events more closely fit his first or second theory? (7 marks)
b) Why might Franco-Russian predominance be 'equally, if not more, formidable to the British Empire' (line 28)? (3 marks)
c) Why might Crowe's policy, if adopted, seem unreasonable to the Germans? (5 marks)

4 Grey's speech to the House of Commons, 3 August 1914
Read the extract on pages 112-3 and answer the following questions.
a) Why was Grey uncertain about the extent of Anglo-French 'obligations' (line 1)? (3 marks)
b) What exactly was at stake, 'from the point of view of British interests' (line 5), if Belgium, Holland, and France fell? (3 marks)
c) What did Grey imply was the main reason necessitating British entry into the war? Explain your answer. (4 marks)

5 'Bravo, Belgium!'
Study the cartoon from *Punch* on page 112 and answer the following questions.
a) Explain how the depictions of Belgium and Germany reinforce the message of the cartoon. (3 marks)
b) How menacing does this representation make the German threat appear? (2 marks)
c) Explain how historically accurate you judge this presentation of events to be. (5 marks)

CHAPTER 6

Conclusion

1 Change and Continuity in British Foreign Policy

We have seen that the period from 1865 to 1914 saw many changes in British foreign policy, not least that, having avoided major war for almost 60 years, Britain entered a Great Power conflict in 1914. At first sight, therefore, it may seem that this period is dominated by change. Yet it is vital to recognise that not everything changed: there are also important continuities. Indeed change and continuity are indissolubly linked. Amidst change there were nevertheless elements of continuity, and alongside substantial continuity there were still some changes.

a) The Economy

A major transformation occurred with Britain's relative economic decline. Britain was the first industrial nation, but it did not remain alone for long. Other countries joined the industrial race, and their superior rates of economic growth steadily whittled away the enormous lead Britain had enjoyed around 1865. The United States became the world's premier economic power, and in Europe Germany's output soon rivalled Britain's. By 1900 Germany was producing more steel than Britain, and by 1914 its overall production was greater.

These economic facts provided a crucial background to foreign policy. The challenge of the United States was too great to be resisted, especially since American might was largely concentrated in the western hemisphere. But German rivalry was much closer at hand and much more threatening to Britain's status as a Great Power, especially when the Kaiser began to build a great navy after 1898, challenging Britannia's traditional capacity to rule the waves.

However, three warnings should be borne in mind, and these emphasise continuity amidst change:
i) We should not exaggerate the degree of Britain's economic decline. Many Britons, enjoying a higher standard of living as the period proceeded and with little knowledge of other countries, were blithely unaware of economic problems - and this was the case not just with the 'man in the street' but with many high-ranking politicians and civil servants. It is easy to understand their lack of concern, for Britain continued to be a highly prosperous country. Indeed *per capita* (i.e. per head of population) she was, as late as 1914, producing virtually as much as the United States and far more than Germany. Admittedly economic problems existed, and in particular imports regularly exceeded exports in value, but this deficit was counterbalanced by the financial strength of the City of London. The profits from 'invisible

exports' (the financial gains from insurance, banking and investments) regularly put the overall 'balance of payments' in the black, not in the red.

ii) Despite relative economic decline, Britain was still a Great Power in 1914 as she had been in 1865. It is impossible to be more exact than this about her 'weight' as a Power. The Royal Navy acted as a protective shield, behind which Britain, alone among the European Powers, could do without conscription. As a result, Britain had not attempted fully to mobilise her resources for war and so had never been fully tested.

iii) Most historians would agree that while economic forces influence human actions they do not actually dictate them. Certainly economic developments, and particularly Anglo-German rivalry, did not make war inevitable. After all, wars break out for particular reasons and because of the actions of politically powerful individuals.

b) Politics

The period 1865-1914 saw substantial political changes in Britain, including the extension of the franchise to include about two-thirds of the adult male population and the limitation of the powers of the House of Lords in 1911 (so that the Upper House could henceforth only delay Bills for two years, not veto them indefinitely). Similarly, the powers of the monarchy declined, so that the monarch became more of a figurehead than an active political participant. Neither Edward VII (1901-10) nor his successor George V (1910-36) had as much impact on foreign policy as Queen Victoria, and her influence had waned considerably as her age increased and the nineteenth century drew to a close. Increasingly the dominant element in parliament was the House of Commons, a majority of whose Members were from middle-class, rather than aristocratic, backgrounds. In short, politics were being fundamentally changed - indeed democratised.

However, the effects of this transformation were slow to make themselves evident for foreign policy, so that there was political continuity as well as change. For example, every foreign secretary from 1865 until 1905, when Sir Edward Grey was appointed, had been a member of the House of Lords; and even Grey followed the practices of his predecessors by, for instance, pleading that foreign policy had to be kept secret to a large extent. The open debate of policy would, he insisted, reveal Britain's secrets to its foreign rivals and thus harm national security; and he was even loath to countenance full cabinet discussion of sensitive issues. Grey was accused by critics of being far too secretive: this had been expected of Derby or Salisbury, but not of a commoner in an era of democratisation. There were even some who said that he was a puppet in the hands of his Foreign Office officials.

i) The Foreign Office

In 1865 the foreign secretary controlled new appointments to the Foreign Office, whose civil servants would be from families personally known to himself or his private secretary. Whereas the rest of Whitehall was being opened up to competitive examination, the Foreign Office - condemned by a Treasury committee as a 'citadel of privilege' - resisted the process. It thus had an essentially amateurish air. Nevertheless, there were changes. Exams were introduced, though only for applicants of whom the minister approved. In addition, the Office grew in size, as the volume of work increased, and it became more professional, with a more specialised division of labour. Increasingly the most senior civil servants were considered not merely clerks - as Lord Salisbury had viewed them - but advisers and experts. A turning point here came around 1900, when - as his girth increased - Salisbury's powers declined. Certainly Grey listened to the views of his staff with great respect.

Yet there are also elements of continuity. Though better informed and more professional, the new generation of Foreign Office men were of the same social background as their predecessors. A greater proportion of successful recruits had now studied at university, but over half had an aristocratic or landed background, the rest coming from the professional middle classes, and all had been to a public school, over 50 per cent being Old Etonians. Nor is it true to say that the Foreign Secretary was their puppet. Grey certainly consulted them and treated them as his social equals, which they were, but he was not 'led astray' by them. There was no conspiracy among the officials to determine British foreign policy. Nor could there have been: at key moments it was the cabinet, not the Foreign Office, which determined policy. This was as true in 1914 as it had been in 1876-9 when the Eastern Crisis assumed menacing proportions, in 1882 when Egypt was invaded, or in 1902 when the Japanese alliance was concluded.

ii) Political Parties

After 1865 the political parties underwent remarkable change, becoming more 'modern' in their form and in their appeal to an increasingly mass electorate. There might be votes to be won from foreign policy, and certainly in the era of Gladstone and Disraeli it seemed that the Liberal and Conservative Parties were poles apart. This was certainly the impression these two parliamentary rivals wished to create: Disraeli stood for national greatness and pursued a policy of asserting Britain's voice in world affairs, and especially in the Empire; Gladstone, on the other hand, was for morality and the application of Christian principles to diplomacy, particularly by means of the Concert of Europe. Newspapers, being mostly either Liberal or Conservative in their allegiance, tended to endorse this divergence. Yet the changes in foreign policy wrought by developments in the party political system were more apparent than real. In practice the differences tended to be essentially matters of style and rhetoric rather than of substance, and after the political falls of Gladstone and Disraeli party differences in foreign policy hardly seemed to exist at all. In the Salisbury era, pragmatism rather than party principle tended to dominate policy. Certainly in 1914 there was substantial unity, although the Conservatives seem to have been wholeheartedly in favour of joining the conflict against Germany, whereas the Liberals hesitated before declaring war. But it probably mattered little which party was in power: there were no marked differences between Liberals and Conservatives, and a bipartisan policy existed. In 1915 they even formed a coalition to prosecute the war together.

iii) Public Opinion

It is virtually impossible for historians to measure public opinion in the period from 1865 to 1914. There were no opinion polls or other methods of gauging what people thought. Nevertheless, public opinion on foreign policy was now more vocal than ever before. Certainly sections of the public made their views felt at times, particularly in 1876 over the Bulgarian Horrors and also in August 1914, when the popular - and totally unrealistic - image of war made many eager for battle. But this is not to say that such outbursts - even if sustained - were representative of the population as a whole. Nor is it at all certain how far government actions were influenced by such demonstrations. What we can be reasonably certain about, however, is that, despite the growth in the electorate and in the circulation of the press, government policy was no more *dictated* by public opinion than it had been in previous periods. In 1876 public outrage at Disraeli's pro-Turk stance merely deterred the Prime Minister from supporting Turkey too openly; and little more than a year later he pressed on with his policy regardless. Nor did uproar at the death of Gordon produce anything more than a tactical change in Gladstone's Sudanese policy. In 1914 the public demonstrations for war did not force the government's hand: they simply confirmed what the majority of the cabinet wanted to do anyway. Hence only a limited - and basically traditional - role should be assigned to public opinion in the policy-making process. Admittedly politicians now waxed more eloquent than ever before about the importance of voters' views, but more often than not they were simply using public opinion to validate a policy which they had decided upon anyway or to avoid a policy of which they disapproved. Salisbury, for instance, pleaded unpopularity with the public as one means of avoiding an Anglo-German alliance. A change in rhetoric should not disguise the continued determination of politicians to control foreign policy.

c) Policies

i) Peace and the Status Quo

Admittedly British policies changed during the period from 1865 to 1914, as circumstances altered. But policies also exhibited an important element of continuity. In particular peace was regarded, broadly, as a national interest, and British politicians tried consistently to avoid major war. Ministers (even Disraeli at the Congress of Berlin) generally stood for negotiation and compromise rather than confrontation and violence. There was continuity of aim because there was continuity of motive. The wish for peace was the result not so much of superior British morality as of profit-and-loss calculation: not only would wars be expensive, but they would disrupt a status quo from which Great Britain was doing very well. Politicians were conservative because Britain and its empire had so much to lose by change. No one recognised this so clearly as Lord Salisbury, but it was at the back of the minds of most ministers. Their country was a satisfied Power. Winston Churchill put the position clearly - and provocatively - when he told cabinet colleagues in 1911 that 'We have got all we want in territory, and our claim to be left in unmolested enjoyment of vast and splendid possessions, mainly acquired by violence, largely maintained by force, often seems less reasonable to others than to us'.

Yet despite the fact that the British tried consistently to avoid major war, their commitment to peace was not absolute. Britain was prepared to fight Russia, for instance in 1878 and 1885, when the defence of India was at stake (or when it was believed to be). Certainly no British government was ever pacifist. Despite professions of peaceful intention, war would be undertaken during 1865-1914, as during earlier and later periods, when there was perceived to be a good enough reason.

ii) Imperial Expansion

Britain did not strive to avoid small wars, especially if opponents were liable to put up little resistance. This was particularly true of imperial clashes. British expansion outside Europe was looked upon as very different, for instance, from German expansion in Europe: the rights of the Zulus and of the Belgians were perceived to be of an entirely different order. The British Empire expanded rapidly in the 1880s and 1890s, and this period of so-called 'New Imperialism' seems to mark a major change in British external policy. Yet it should be recognised that most politicians, and especially Gladstone and Salisbury, did not positively desire to expand the Empire. On the contrary, they joined the Scramble for Africa only reluctantly. Far to be preferred, they judged, was the 'informal empire' of the mid-nineteenth century; but since other European Powers insisted on annexing territory, Britain had to do the same in order to preserve at least some of its dominance. A change in policy thus obscures continuity of intention. Not surprisingly, many historians interpret the outburst of territorial acquisition in Africa and elsewhere as essentially a defeat for Britain: her power was patently insufficient to keep rivals at bay. Formal empire over a relatively small area was a poor substitute for informal dominance over a much greater one.

iii) Europe

Lord Salisbury once said that 'We are fish'. By this he meant that Britain was a global Power and that Britons were more concerned with the wider world across the oceans than with the nearby continent of Europe. This was true throughout the period from 1865 to 1914. We do not have to accept the exaggerated notion that Britain was in 'splendid isolation' from other European Powers at the end of the nineteenth century to accept that entry into a major European war in 1914 was a significant change. But was it a complete transformation of policy?

The British tended to have an ambivalent attitude towards Europe, wishing to be involved and to protect their interests, but also to maintain a free hand. Disraeli had intervened provocatively in the 1870s, with his responses to the 'war in sight' crisis and to the Berlin Memorandum, and Gladstone also pursued an active European policy. But no government made any irrevocable commitments and, despite negotiations, no alliance was signed with a European partner. Neither the Entente with France (1904) nor that with Russia (1907) committed Britain to fight in a continental war. Moral obligations to France there may have been, and certainly the synchronisation of Anglo-French naval and military plans marked a definite change in foreign policy. But Britain was still uncommitted when the July Crisis broke. We can thus see an important strand of continuity in foreign policy from 1865 to 1914.

Admittedly Britain opted to join the war in August 1914, a decision which marks an important change, but even this was not a complete break with the past. Britain's traditional policy had been to prevent any single Power becoming too dominant in Europe: if this did occur, Britain itself might not be safe from invasion. A Balance of Power had therefore to be maintained. This had been British policy at the time of Napoleon a century earlier and during the reign of Louis XIV two centuries before. Entry into what the British called 'the Kaiser's war' was therefore both a startlingly new departure in foreign policy but also, from a longer perspective, completely traditional.

2 Serving the National Interest?

We have seen that there was both change and continuity in foreign policy from 1865 to 1914. But was there consistency in that British governments constantly strove to promote the national interest? They generally said that this was their aim, but did they actually do so? Formulated more simply, did Britain pursue the 'right' policies?

Historians sometimes cannot resist intriguing questions - even when it is impossible to answer them satisfactorily! The issue of the calibre and correctness of British foreign policy will surely be debated endlessly. Should Disraeli have jettisoned support for Turkey? Did he exaggerate the threat from Russia? Should Gladstone have resigned rather than invade Egypt? If Salisbury had adopted Chamberlain's idea of an alliance with Germany, might the results have been beneficial? What would have happened if Asquith's government had attempted to stay out of the Great War? This last question is particularly important, especially since the consequences of Britain's entry into the First World War were to be so profound. Yet such questions, though fascinating, are infuriatingly difficult to answer with any hope of correctness. Since even the best-informed historians are able to do no more than speculate about such questions, perhaps we should stick with what did happen rather than with what might have happened.

However, because a number of historians have chosen to enter this dangerous territory, it would not be realistic for those studying British foreign policy between 1865 and 1914 to avoid the issue altogether. In particular, it is necessary to comment on those critics who have insisted that British foreign policy served the interests not of the whole nation but of a small clique and that it did so because this small group was actually able to control governments. For example, many writers have insisted that capitalists and financiers produced the Scramble for Africa. It has been argued that first they invested funds in Africa and then, to protect their investments, they persuaded governments to establish formal control. Similar arguments have been put forward to explain the First World War and Britain's role in it. It has been claimed that European Powers, and particularly Britain and Germany, were cut-throat competitors striving for economic supremacy; and that, in order to achieve total dominance, industrialists urged their respective governments to war, after which they could seize the economic spoils. The major problem with such theories is the total lack of persuasive direct evidence to support them. In addition, Britain and Germany were becoming increasingly interdependent economically. Britain was almost exclusively dependent on German chemical products and scientific instruments, while Germany was a huge market for the British textile industry. In addition, industrialists in 1914 were convinced - partly because of Norman Angell's *The Great Illusion* (1909) - that an Anglo-German war would be an economic catastrophe.

Similarly, little credence can be given to the notion that a few Foreign Office officials, implacably and unreasonably anti-German, plotted to bring Britain into the war in 1914. British foreign policy did not always exhibit clear-sighted awareness of all European issues: ministers and politicians were often muddled, confusing prestige with honour, legitimate interests with selfish gains, and fears with realities, but the very complexity of the foreign policy debate in Britain gives the lie to such simple assertions. Foreign policy was not a conspiracy, it was - and is, to us as historians - a process of endless complexity and fascination.

Working on 'Conclusion'

Far more important than compiling a detailed set of notes on this chapter is ensuring that you have thought about the fundamental issues raised. It is very difficult to consider the period from 1865 to 1914 as a whole, and so it is worthwhile asking how far (i) the 'realities behind diplomacy' (i.e. the British economy and politics) and (ii) foreign policies themselves actually changed. The chapter is based on the view that the best way of discerning change is also to search for continuity. But rather than accepting the arguments put forward in the preceding pages, which you should treat as merely a guide, you can now attempt to formulate your own ideas, using the information provided in earlier chapters.

Chronological Table

1856		Congress of Paris, after Crimean War
1865		Death of Palmerston
1866		Austro-Prussian War
1868		Liberals returned to power under Gladstone
1869		Opening of the Suez Canal
1870	July	Start of Franco-Prussian War
	October	Russians repudiated Black Sea Clauses of Treaty of Paris
1871		Unification of Germany; Treaty of Frankfurt imposed on France
1872		Gladstone accepted arbitration over the *Alabama* dispute
1874		Conservatives, under Disraeli, won power
1875	May	'War in Sight' crisis
		Disraeli spent £4m on 44 per cent of shares in Suez Canal Company
	December	Revolt of Bosnia and Herzegovina against Turks
	30 December	Andrassy Note to the Sultan
1876	May	Berlin Memorandum; Turkish revolution, Abdul Hamid as sultan
	June	Massacre of 12,000 in 'Bulgarian Horrors'
		Gladstone came out of semi-retirement
	November	Conference at Constantinople
1876		Queen Victoria became Empress of India
1877	April	Start of Russo-Turkish War
1878	March,	Treaty of San Stefano (with a 'Big Bulgaria')
		British troops sent to Malta; resignation of Derby as Foreign Secretary and appointment of Salisbury
		Congress of Berlin (with a smaller Bulgaria)
1879		Anglo-Afghan War
		Zulu War
		Austro-German alliance
1880		Election victory for Gladstone, after Midlothian campaigns
	September	Naval demonstration off Albania to coerce Turkey
	December	Boers declared Transvaal a republic

1881		League of Three Emperors (Germany, Austria and Russia) - also known as *Dreikaiserbund*
		First Boer War
	April	Convention of Pretoria
	September	Military rebellion in Egypt
1882	June	50 Europeans killed in Alexandria
	August	Gladstone's invasion of Egypt
		Triple Alliance (Germany, Austria and Italy)
1884		London Convention; Bechuanaland annexed
	March	Siege of Khartoum began
1885	February	General Gordon found dead in Khartoum
	March	Penjdeh incident; Russian army defeated Afghans
	April	British withdrawal from the Sudan
		Bulgarian crisis over Eastern Roumelia; effective end of League of Three Emperors
1887		Reinsurance Treaty (Germany and Russia)
		Mediterranean Agreements (Britain, Italy and Austria)
1889		Naval Defences Act; Britain adopted the 'two power standard'
1890		Fall of Bismarck
1894		Franco-Russian alliance
		Britain annexed Uganda
	March	Resignation of Gladstone
1895		Massacre of Armenians in Constantinople and Asia Minor
		Jameson Raid in the Transvaal
1896		Further Armenian massacres
		Anglo-American dispute over Venezuela; arbitration accepted
1897		Mediterranean Agreements lapsed
1898	September	Kitchener's victory at Omdurman
		Fashoda Incident; France backed down
		Start of German naval-building programme
1899	October	Second Boer War began
1900		'Boxer Rebellion' against foreigners in China.
		Lansdowne succeeded Salisbury as Foreign Secretary
1902		Anglo-Japanese alliance
		End of Boer War
		Resignation of Salisbury as Prime Minister
1904		Start of Russo-Japanese War

		Entente Cordiale
1905	March	Kaiser landed at Tangier; first Moroccan Crisis
	December	Sir Edward Grey became Liberal Foreign Secretary
1906		Algeçiras Conference, ending Moroccan Crisis. Launch of HMS *Dreadnought*; new phase in naval race
1907		Anglo-Russian Entente
1908		Austria annexed Bosnia and Herzegovina
1911		First Balkan War (Balkan League against Turkey)
	July	German gunboat arrived at Agadir; second Moroccan Crisis
1912		Haldane's (unsuccessful) mission to Germany
1913		Anglo-French naval agreement; Great Britain to defend French coastline
	May	Treaty of London, ending first Balkan War Second Balkan War (Serbia against Bulgaria), ended by Treaty of Bucharest
1914	January-June	Better Anglo-German relations
	28 June	Assassination of Archduke Franz Ferdinand at Sarajevo
	5 July	Germany's 'blank cheque' to Austria
	23 July	Austria's ultimatum to Serbia
	1 August	Germany declared war on Russia
	3 August	Germany declared war on France; Belgium called for British help
	4 August	Britain declared war on Germany

Further Reading

This book complements two others in the *Access to History* series. Students are therefore advised to consult **John Lowe,** *Rivalry and Accord: International Relations 1870-1914* (Hodder and Stoughton, 1988) for the European background and **Frank McDonough,** *The British Empire 1815-1914* (Hodder and Stoughton, 1994) for a treatment of imperial affairs.

1 General texts

There are a number of illuminating general studies of British foreign policy in the nineteenth century. Two of the most recent are **Muriel Chamberlain,** *'Pax Britannica'? British Foreign Policy 1789-1914* (Longman, 1988), an excellent readable introduction, and **C.J. Bartlett,** *Defence and Diplomacy: Britain and the Great Powers, 1815-1914* (Manchester University Press, 1993). Among the 'heavier' works are **Kenneth Bourne,** *Victorian Foreign Policy* (Oxford, 1970); **P. Hayes,** *Modern British Foreign Policy,* 2 vols. (Black, 1975 and 1978); **C.J. Lowe,** *The Reluctant Imperialists: British Foreign Policy 1878-1902,* 2 vols. (Routledge, 1967); and **C.J. Lowe and M.L. Dockrill,** *The Mirage of Power, 1902-1922,* 3 vols. (Routledge, 1972). A stimulating and well-written survey of background influences on foreign policy is provided by **Paul Kennedy,** *The Realities Behind Diplomacy* (Fontana, 1981). The essays in **Keith Wilson** (ed), *British Foreign Secretaries and Foreign Policy* (Croom Helm, 1987) are worth reading. A very sound general textbook, which relates external policy to other issues, is **Richard Shannon,** *The Crisis of Imperialism, 1865-1915* (Granada, 1976)

2 Gladstone, Disraeli and Salisbury

Valuable works on Gladstone and Disraeli include numerous biographical studies, especially **Robert Blake,** *Disraeli* (Eyre & Spottiswoode, 1966). **R. Millman,** *Britain and the Eastern Question* (Clarendon Press, 1979) is among the best of numerous studies of this issue. Much older, but also valuable, is **R.W. Seton-Watson,** *Disraeli, Gladstone and the Eastern Question* (Macmillan, 1935), which is far more critical of Disraeli.

On 'Splendid Isolation' and its demise, two books are particularly valuable: **J.A.S. Grenville,** *Lord Salisbury and Foreign Policy* (Athlone Press, 1964) and **Paul Kennedy,** *The Rise of Anglo-German Antagonism* (Allen & Unwin, 1980).

3 First World War

For the origins of the First World War, students are advised to consult **Zara Steiner,** *Britain and the Origins of the First World War* (Macmillan, 1977), which is detailed but accessible, and **F.H. Hinsley (ed),** *The Foreign Policy of Sir Edward Grey* (Cambridge, 1977). There is a stimulating essay on Britain's entry into the war in **Keith Wilson (ed),** *Decisions for War, 1914* (UCL Press, 1995). On the Foreign Office, **Zara Steiner** *The Foreign Office and Foreign Policy, 1898-1914* (Cambridge University Press, 1969) is extremely valuable.

4 Source Material

Bourne's volume contains a selection of documents. The second volume by **Lowe** comprises source material, as does the third volume by **Lowe and Dockrill.** A very short selection is provided by **Bartlett.** Also important - though not for the faint-hearted! - are the 11 volumes of *British documents on the Origins of the War, 1898-1914,* edited by **Gooch and Temperley** (1927-38).

Index

Afghanistan 10, 18, 32, 47-8, 59, 63-4
Agadir Crisis 104-6
Alabama 15
Andrassy Note 17
Anglo-Japanese Alliance (1902) 85-7
Armenian massacres 76-7
Asquith, Herbert 109-11, 114, 127
Balance of Power 3, 12, 46, 104, 115, 126
Balkan wars 11, 107-8
Baring, Sir Evelyn 57
Belgium 15, 111-12, 114
Berlin Memorandum (1876) 18-19, 31, 35
Bismarck, Otto von 9, 11, 14-18, 27, 29, 45, 53, 64, 70, 74, 98
Boer Wars 10, 12, 49, 81-2, 84
Bosnia 9, 17, 27, 107
Boxer Rebellion 79
Bright, John 3, 14, 54-6, 62
British economy 1-2, 6-7, 36, 97, 121-22
Bulgaria 26-7
  Horrors 9, 19-22, 25, 124
  1885 Crisis 73

Chamberlain, Joseph 50, 60, 81-4, 108, 127
China 10, 71, 79, 85
Churchill, Winston 100, 106, 125
Cobden, Richard 3, 14, 18
Concert of Europe 3, 9-10, 12, 43, 45-6, 56, 77, 108
Conference of Berlin (1884) 59
Congress of Berlin (1878) 9, 11, 17, 27-32, 73, 125

Congress of Paris (1856) 6, 8, 15
Convention of Pretoria (1881) 50
Crimean War 3, 5
Crowe, Eyre 103-4, 110
Cyprus 28

Derby, Lord 18, 23-4, 26, 31, 36, 48, 63
Disraeli, Benjamin 9-10, 14-15, 70, 97, 123-7
  as Prime Minister 1874-80 16-37
  compared with Gladstone 36, 42, 60-3
Dreadnoughts 99-100, 102

Eastern Question 4-5, 17-31, 76-7
Egypt 10, 16, 18, 52-8, 75, 78, 87-8
Electoral reform 7-8, 36, 122
Elliot, Sir Henry 22, 24
Entente Cordiale (1904) 10, 87-8, 90, 101, 126

Fashoda 78, 79, 84, 87
Ferdinand, Franz 108
Foreign Office 122-3, 127-8
Franco-Russian alliance (1894) 75, 78
Frankfurt, Treaty of (1871) 15, 64
Frere, Sir Bartle 33, 48

Gladstone, William 9, 70, 75-6, 123-7
  Prime Minister in 1868-74 15
  and Bulgarian Horrors 20, 22, 25
  and Midlothian campaigns 33, 42-3

Prime Minister in 1880-85
    43-59
Prime Minister in 1886 and
    1892-4   60
compared with Disraeli   36,
    60-3
Gordon, General Charles   57-8,
    63, 78, 124
Granville, Lord   48, 53-4
Grey, Sir Edward   12, 102-7,
    109-12, 112-13, 115

Haldane, Lord   106
Hartington, Lord   49, 53-4
Hayashi   86

Jameson raid   81
Japan   10, 71, 79, 85-7

Kitchener, Lord   78
Kruger, Paul   50, 81-2

Lansdowne, Lord   82, 84, 86-7,
    102
Lloyd George, David   103, 105,
    108, 111, 115
London Convention (1884)   50

Mahdi   57, 78
Mediterranean Agreements
    (1887)   74, 77-8, 89
Midlothian campaigns   42-3,
Moroccan Crises   11
    in 1905   101-2
    in 1911 (Agadir)   104-6

Naval Defence Act (1889)   75
Naval Race
    with Russia   10, 75, 86
    with Germany   11, 87, 98-101
Nicholas II   77

Omdurman (1898)   78

Palmerston, Lord   1-2, 14
Panslavism   4

Penjdeh incident (1885)   48, 59,
    62
Persia   10, 79, 88
Plevna   24-5

Reinsurance Treaty (1887)   46,
    74, 78
Rhodes, Cecil   50, 81
Rosebery, Lord   60
Russo-Japanese war   87-8

Salisbury, Lord   10, 23, 26, 29,
    31, 52, 115, 123-7
as Prime Minister in 1885-92
    64, 70-6
as Prime Minister in
    1895-1902   76-85
San Stefano, Treaty of (1878)
    26-7, 34, 73
Serbia   18-19, 27, 107-8
Social Darwinism   93-4, 105,
    114
South Africa   33, 48-52, 64, 81-2
Spencer, Herbert   94
Splendid Isolation   10, 72, 82, 89
Steevens, George   94-5
Sudan   56-9, 78
Suez Canal   16, 18, 53-5

Three Emperors' League
    (1873)   16-18, 27, 30
    (1881)   32, 46, 73
Triple Alliance (1882)   46, 73-4,
    76, 82, 89
Triple Entente (1907)   88-9, 90,
    115, 126

USA   6-7, 12, 80, 114, 121

Venezuela   80
Victoria, Queen   1, 17, 19, 24,
    44, 57, 60, 82, 122

Wilhelm II   11, 71, 78, 98, 101,
    108, 121